THE END
OF INNOVATION
IN ARCHITECTURE

Computer-generated realization of the Millennium Experience Dome (Richard Rogers Partnership)

Chorley Handford/Hayes Davidson

Inside Covers
Kisho Kurokawa: Ehime Science Museum. Sketches from his major retrospective exhibition at the Maison de la Culture du Japon à Paris
Cover
Earth Atmosphere, photo ESA
Inserts: Top: Coop Himmelb(l)au; Bottom: Morphosis

NA
NEW ARCHITECTURE

THE END
OF INNOVATION
IN ARCHITECTURE

Rem Koolhaas, Winning Entry for the Illinois Institute of Technology Campus Center Design Competition

OPPOSITE: Video screens and lights in Shibuya District, Tokyo. Photo Alex Papadakis

ANDREAS PAPADAKIS PUBLISHER

NEW ARCHITECTURE
Number 2, 1998

Head Office
Kilbees Farm, Hatchet Lane
Windsor, Berks SL4 2EH
United Kingdom

UK Tel. 013 44 88 20 40
UK Fax 013 44 88 20 41
International Tel. +44 13 44 88 20 40
International Fax +44 13 44 88 20 41
e-mail papadakis@btinternet.com

Editor-in-Chief
Andreas Papadakis

Design by: Andrea Bettella and
Mario Bettella of Artmedia
Contributing Editors and Correspondents:
Botond Bognar, Luigi Croce,
Lois Papadopoulos
Assistant: Alex Papadakis

NEW ARCHITECTURE is available by subscription
and in bookshops worldwide. Subscription rates for
six numbers (including p&p): £90.00/US$135.
Individual issues are available at £17.50/US$27.50

Printed and bound in Singapore

NEW ARCHITECTURE is an international journal of contemporary thought and practice in architecture and urban design. Designed with flair, it is edited and produced by a talented, experienced team that has excellent relations not only with the profession, academics and the schools but also with thinkers and world leaders who shape the society in which we live.

NEW ARCHITECTURE features survey and critical articles and presents the work and writings not only of all the top international architects but also of the young and innovative who have not yet made their mark. It looks critically at current directions, irrespective of stylistic and theoretical considerations, and explores each issue in depth raising all the important questions posed by the developing role of architecture in the world today.

NEW ARCHITECTURE carries up-to-date information and critical comment, and offers a platform for discussion on what is happening now in the worlds of Architectural Theory and Design, Urbanism, Design, Design Technology, Landscape, Interior Design, and the Fine Arts; it has features on significant competitions, exhibitions, conferences and books, and a special section devoted to the schools.

contents

Eric Owen Moss

Kisho Kurokawa in Paris for the opening of the first of his two exhibitions there

Javier Rojas Rodriguez, joint organizer of the Make and Remake *Conference in Monterrey, Mexico*

CONFERENCES AND EVENTS

We are grateful to the organizers and participants of the following conferences and events for their support and for valuable discussions:
MAKE AND REMAKE in Monterrey, Mexico , with Hiromi Fujii, Farshid Moussavi, Andreas Papadakis, Peter Pran, Dagmar Richter, Michael Sorkin, Mark Wigley and Elia Zenghelis, conference organized by **Javier Rojas Rodriguez** and **Laura Chiovatero** with the help of **Sergio Blasquez Mier**, **Carmen Ivetto Romo**, **Rolando Martinez** and **Paola Venegas Chapluk**.
PRE BIENAL in Buenos Aires with Mario Botta, Sir Norman Foster, Kenneth Frampton, Vittorio Gregotti, Rafael de la Hoz, Joseph Kleihues, Ricardo Legorreta, Andreas Papadakis, Cesar Pelli, Wolf Prix, Franco Purini, Zhang Qinnan and Terence Riley, organized by **Jorge Glusberg**.
EUROPEAN ASSOCIATION FOR JAPANESE STUDIES, Budapest, Hungary, organized by **Dr. Judit Hidasi**, and especially the Urban and Environmental Studies convened by **Nicolas Fiévé** and **Uta Hohn**.
KISHO KUROKAWA: METABOLISM 1960-1975 at the Pompidou Centre, Paris and **KISHO KUROKAWA RETROSPECTIVE** at the Maison de la culture du Japon, Paris.
THESSALONIKI CULTURAL CAPITAL OF EUROPE: the organizers of the special events and especially **Dimitri Fatouros** and **Lois Papadopoulos**.

ACKNOWLEDGMENTS

The Editor wishes to thank the following: Professor **Harold Bloom** for inspiration from his revised and expanded volume, *The Anxiety of Influence*, Oxford, 1997; **John Horgan** for permission to extract from his highly readable and informative bestselling book, *The End of Science* (Little Brown and Company); Professor **Francis Fukuyama** and the Social Market Foundation for permission to publish extracts from his lectures delivered at Brasenose College, Oxford and published in full under the title *The End of Order* by the Centre for Collectivist Studies; **Lebbeus Woods** for responding at such short notice; **Botond Bognar** who succeeds in conveying a vision of Japan enriched by his own inside information and photographs. **Eric Owen Moss** for permission to extract from the preliminary version of his book *Gnostic Architecture* (to be published later this year by The Monacelli Press); **Michael Sorkin** for allowing us to present his work and **Andrei Vovk** for putting together and designing the feature; **Gisela Hossmann** for her essay on Kurt Schwitters' Hanover *Merzbau* and *Ursonate* to accompany Jack Ox's "From Merz to Ur" and to **Jack Ox** for permission to reproduce her work; the **Pompidou Centre** for material on the **Bruce Nauman** exhibition; the **Museum of London** for material on Bedlam from their excellent exhibition: *Bedlam, Custody, Care and Cure*;

Jorge Glusberg, Director of the Museum of Fine Arts in Buenos Aires, for providing material on the exhibition of Contemporary Italian Silver; and to **Michael Hensel** of the Architectural Association and **Dr. Mohsen Mostafavi**, its Chairman, for their help in producing this number's Schools feature. And finally we would like to thank our illustrious Editorial Board for their continuing support.

HRH The Prince of Wales with Andreas Papadakis at Poundbury

Sir Norman Foster at the Pre Bienal in Buenos Aires with his wife Dr. Elena Ochoa and Arq. Manuel de la Hoz, past president of the UIA

Wolf Prix in Buenos Aires

The End of Innovation

Andreas Papadakis

Daedalus, one of the earliest recorded architects in Ancient Greece murdered his talented student and nephew, Talos, by pushing him from the top of Athene's temple on the Acropolis. He did so purely to protect his own position as the most innovative architect of his age. `He was, by definition, at the cutting edge of architecture[1] but even then, right at the outset, he sensed that there are finite limits to human achievement and by his very action predicted the end of innovation in architecture. Despite his tumultuous career he succeeded in completing a large number of commissions, from King Minos's palace in Crete to fine buildings in Sicily.

Today, architects have to contend not only with one and a half million or so contemporaries but also a long lineage of illustrious predecessors. How, then, is it possible for the architect to express his individuality? And is he alone in his preoccupations?

In his recently revised highly influential essay *The Anxiety of Influence*, Harold Bloom, professor of English literature at Yale, turned his considerable analytical powers to the end of innovation in poetry. He is concerned with just this problem and concludes that all the great poetry that could be written has already been written. His poet is essentially a tragic figure faced with 'the embarrassments of a tradition grown too wealthy to need anything more,' who can assert his individuality only by defying, or deliberately misreading his predecessors.

The entries for this year's prestigious Booker prize have been criticized for cultural fatigue and a flight into the past. According to one of the judges, Jason Cowley, 'the contemporary novelist in search of an elusive originality must feel as if he is at the end of something; that he is living over-historically, part of a tradition which has cannily foreseen the important work as yet unwritten.'[2] The submission of Ted Hughes, Britain's poet laureate, for best poem of the year is a *reworking* of Ovid's *Actaeon*. And further afield, a Russian literary judge of the new regime publicly laments the failure to find a new Tolstoy whilst castigating the prizewinner as a man of the past.

The question of the anxiety of influence and the limits to human invention concerns other disciplines too. In his much discussed book, *The End of Science*, John Horgan claims that it is extremely unlikely that research in pure science will provide any major rethinks. It is more probable that it will be limited to tinkering with existing theories and to the applied sciences.

Architecture is hardly immune from such considerations. The innovative architect is right to be concerned with whether his design concept can or indeed should be free from the influence of the past.

 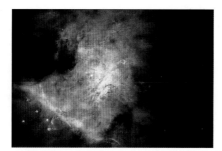 

OPPOSITE: Daedalus; LEFT: Video screen wall in Tokyo; CENTRE: Orion Nebula (photo ESA); RIGHT: Peter Eisenman, Church for the Year 2000

After all, architects can legitimately claim that the heritage of the past belongs to them and that dead architects cannot claim ownership but only participation. To paraphrase Shelley, 'Architects of all ages contribute to one great architecture perpetually in progress.' In other words, the development of architecture is a linear progression where art, knowledge and skills are added cumulatively through the ages so that today's architect takes his place in the progression and contributes incrementally; a concept to which Léon Krier and traditional architects of today would subscribe.

But this cosy view of architecture was already shattered when the early moderns grasped the creative freedom of industrial technology and the new forms it offered. Today, architects are responding once again to the new products and concepts of the industrial world and are turning for inspiration to what has been dubbed the 'information age.' Many are obsessed with innovation and are looking for ways to express it in both form and materials and, in form at least, recent advances in the applied sciences and technology are coming to the rescue of the innovative architect. Modern electronic technology and advanced computational techniques permit the design of complex shapes; and the refinement of video and liquid crystal technology offers innumerable new opportunities. Wolf Prix says that he would rather die than not be free to innovate and openly rejoices in his 'freedom from the box.' In his church for the year 2000 Peter Eisenman not only substitutes liquid crystal displays for stained glass, but his design principle is itself based on the two-dimensional crystalline structure offered by the medium.

Far from being the enemy of the designing architect, the new giant video/liquid crystal screens now appearing on the facades of new buildings offer opportunities undreamed of by modern pioneers in their search for transparency. Buildings are being turned inside out and, with their new accessibility, form an integral part of the city. Diller and Scofidio's installations provide a glimpse of what is to come. It is in Japan that the quest – and indeed the necessity – for innovation is at its maximum. Vitruvius's *firmitas* is becoming irrelevant as buildings are torn down after just a few years. The word *ephemeral* is treated with the respect of its original meaning: that which fulfils its purpose. And that purpose is being fulfilled more and more rapidly leading to an architecture perpetually at the cutting edge.[3]

The question still remains whether this is a satisfactory route in establishing a stake in true originality.

1 In more senses than one since he is often credited with the invention of the saw. 2 Jason Cowley, 'Fictional Failure,' *Prospect*, December 1997. 3 These points will be developed further in the forthcoming number of NEW ARCHITECTURE on Japan.

Lebbeus Woods

The Crisis of Innovation

This is the way the world ends,
This is the way the world ends,
Not with a bang,
But with a whimper.

T.S. Eliot
The Hollow Men (1925)

It is not entirely clear to me why Andreas Papadakis has taken up 'the end of innovation' as a prospect architects should, at the end of the century and the millennium, consider. But I am glad he has. By raising the issue he calls into question an idea too long taken for granted and long overdue for criticism. I'm not referring only to the idea of innovation-as-progress contained within post-modernist critiques of modernism, which are not only highly competitive, thus antagonistic from the start, but also too quick to consign innovation to a historical scheme that deprives it of any possible *poetic* vitality today. What is needed instead is a fresh look at innovation as a force that may still serve humanist, if not modernist, ends in spite of all post-modernist disdain for both.

For thoughtful observers today, innovation has a host of negative aspects. It is first of all associated with exploitation, chiefly because of the manipulation of ever-changing fashions and trends which yields celebrity and notoriety for a few clever self-promoters, and always translates into someone's financial gain. Or, the exploitation of the global marketplace by the mass-marketing of new products, 'new' meaning everything from new-everywhere to new-only-there, in the 'developing markets' of Eastern Europe, Asia, Africa, South America, which are desperate for signs of 'first world' status, however regressive, outdated, or banal these may be.

Another negative for innovation is its continuing alliance with big business, the multi-national corporate structure whose financial machinations continue as they have throughout the nineteenth and twentieth centuries to run roughshod over political, ecological, and cultural landscapes in pursuit of their own interests. Few would disagree today that

the various national governments are not to some considerable extent surrogates of the most powerful international corporations, and have to the same degree become identified by and with their interests, often at the expense of concerns for which they are the supposed stewards. The battle over the European Union, to cite only the most current example, centres on the issue of a common European currency and related economic matters – social and cultural issues are entirely subsumed in financial ones. Innovation, in this and other similar schemata – like the controversial GATT treaty in the United States – is only the measure of a market 'edge' that determines big winners and losers in the games of global capital.

But the most damning aspect of innovation comes from its tricky relationship with the idea of progress. "Progress," Herbert Marcuse wrote, "becomes quantitative and tends to *delay indefinitely the turn from quantity to quality* [author's italics] – that is, the emergence of new modes of existence with new modes of reason and freedom." Quantity is mathematically certain, the main ingredient of the 'bottom line' profit margin of corporate enterprise, whereas quality is negotiable, manageable, manipulable, a kind of phantom that has no specific place in ledgers, but is nonetheless subject to them.

However, many promises made at the beginning of this century – the century of modernization – were qualitative and foretold of broad human progress that would result from discoveries of science and technology, applied through art and design. Many of the quantitative promises were kept: bigger, faster, more complex have certainly been achieved in modern societies. But they have often been achieved at the cost of concepts such as social justice and universal human suffrage that have also been promised, a reward to the great masses of industrial workers who have actually built modern technological society. Even worse, the effects of global and regional wars, of ecological disasters, of rising unemployment and declining environmental quality in many cities, of diminishing purchasing power of most wage earners, of reduced health care and educational opportunities, and other erosions of the quality of life for many, have given rise to political and cultural reaction, which threatens the hard-won gains of modern society. Resurgent nationalism and regional chauvinism are all that are left out of the globalization game. Progress for some has translated into regress for many.

Under the duress of fear or disillusionment, it is extremely difficult for "new modes of existence with new modes of reason and freedom" to emerge. They, of course, cannot emerge of their own accord, but only as a result of a conscious, and concerted, human action. In their place today, however, much innovation is directed towards quantitative goals, managed by the corporate stewards of modernization, and results in the creation only of new modes of entertainment, distraction, and consumer passivity. *Circus et panem*,[1] technocratic style.

Art and design, and architecture in particular, because it unifies them, have been a significant part of both the promise and failure of modernization, at least in qualitative terms. There has been plenty of innovation by architects, from the beginning of the century up to the present moment, but it has had less and less to do with improving the general quality of human existence, as the decline of the most innovative architects' interest in housing clearly demonstrates. Today, following the general cultural trend, the greatest innovations are in museums, which, together with cinemas, theme park buildings, libraries, and concert halls, can arguably be considered, from the public's point of view, as places of high-end, up-scale entertainment, and in many cases themselves as a secondary source of entertainment, when experienced through television, magazines and books. The point here is not that these are unworthy cultural productions, but just the opposite: that they represent perhaps all too well a society that has shifted its qualitative concerns from broad improvements in the human condition to narrow ones, a society in which, it is only fair to say, innovation has been subsumed almost entirely by the quantification not simply of culture, but of the human condition itself.

When the modern era was still innocent of itself, the work produced by the Bauhaus, the Suprematist and Constructivist, De Stijl, Futurist, Expressionist, and other, independent architects was vivid with a power to rally and coalesce industrial society's emerging energies into a new collective/urban world, one that relied without apology upon materialism and the idea of continuous innovation. What was needed, they argued, was a new architecture and urbanism, a new materiality and order of materiality that were required, not to complete, nor, even less, to 'express' post facto the processes of radical change, but to actively initiate them. Only when new types of space were constructed, offering the potential to be inhabited in new ways, could the ethics, politics and culture of modernity be defined, implemented, and realized. Even before modern social institutions were well defined, as in post-World War I Germany and Russia, architects brazenly assumed a leading role, becoming the vanguard of a better society they believed would surely come.

Pulsing beneath the architects' audacity was their faith in the capacity of people (inspired, perhaps, by their example) to create their own destinies, and the means by which to attain them. Sant'Elia's statement, "Each generation must build

its own city," could not have been made without his conviction that each generation would want to be as innovative as he perceived his own to be, and that architecture could be the primary instrument of effecting social change. But as the century nears its end, it is very clear that neither has proved to be the case.

The problematic inherent in optimistic projections about the relationship of architecture to social change and political power[2] is that the most innovative architects chose to be sanguine, whereas the regimes they imagined themselves allied with, such as those of revolutionary Russia or post-war America, treated architects and architecture more as pawns than protagonists.

Eventually, architects became aware of the fact that the various institutions behind modernization were less interested in architectural expressions of social ideals than in tangible, quantitative results. After all, by the mid-forties, the early, hairy days of the founding of socialist and capitalist societies, when innovative designs were useful as instruments of propaganda and persuasion (and rarely built), were over. What was needed then were large-scale works, more engineering than architecture, that fulfilled grand post-World War II economic schemes that led eventually to 'globalization,' and also special, symbolic buildings that reassured all concerned that culture was not being ground to dust under a new form of totalization. The focus today on innovative buildings of this latter type speaks more than anything of architects' acceptance of the terms of this new stage of modernization's harsher reality.

Where once the most innovative architects felt confident enough of their ethical footing to propose designs that took the lead in transforming existing ways of living, today's leading architects concern themselves primarily with recasting in new forms familiar and already established ideas of social life and experience. Confronted with the dramatic and sometimes tumultuous social changes now affecting cities, these architects demur, preferring instead to address in their work high-profile building types where innovation is confined to formal, not existential, aspects of design. Innovation has, as a result, become synonymous with fashion, sensation and celebrity, and no longer with the goal of initiating, and of leading, social change.

In reaction, the younger generation of architects today, idealistic as ever and therefore wishing to avoid the shallowness of being mere stylists, often consider the making of new types of forms anathema, a mark only of the hubris of architects. Far from being considered as a means of changing the human condition for the better, the invention of radically new forms and spaces seems to many socially irresponsible. Innovation, therefore, is justifiable only within the framework of the already known and accepted. Rem Koolhaas, whose ideas about architecture and urbanism are both revealing and influential, has claimed that in the early days of the century, the heroic position was one of rebellion against convention, against the established norms of society. Today, however, the heroic position is one of going along with what he calls 'the inevitable,' of accepting and working within the mainstream.[3]

Implicit in this statement is a resigned assessment of the status and the state of contemporary architecture, both of which have fallen far in their impact on and relation with today's most pressing social, cultural and political conditions.

And it is difficult to argue, in practical terms, with this assessment. Looking back over the century, it is painfully obvious that all the bold social innovations initiated at its beginning, which architects sought to lead with their innovative designs, have failed, leaving in the end no socially cohering ideals for architects to codify in terms of urban space and form. Indeed, the boldest innovations of modern architecture itself – in mass housing and urban planning – failed to the same degree, and for the same reasons. Lacking any ideals of social progress to coalesce in great building projects, architects today do not have the confidence, the will or the desire to lead in the innovation "of new modes of existence with new modes of reason and freedom." Because they have convinced themselves that they only serve a society over which they have no control, and in which their authority is greatly diminished, they wait dutifully for orders from further up the economic chain of command. As Rem Koolhaas has also noted, "for their thoughts to be mobilized architects depend on the provocations of others – clients, individual or institutional."[4]

Architects no longer feel responsible for initiating social change through their designs; nor for their own narrowing of scope within its dynamics; nor even for the end of innovation, as they might once have conceived it. They have returned this responsibility to the individuals and institutions who held it before the beginning of this century, before the advent of modernity, with its promises of empowering the great numbers of people through new social, political and cultural institutions. In this sense, innovation has indeed come to an end. Tragically, I would say, and almost completely.

My 'almost' is of course the fragile thread on which my own work, indeed my very belief in architecture, precariously hangs. Whether the thread connecting architecture to the more universal human condition breaks in my case is merely a matter of personal concern. However, if it should break at the weak points it now exhibits for the present society generally, the results will be catastrophic, and probably irreversible.

I will close with a brief reflection made a year ago,[5] which could be seen as a cross-section through this thread.

"Whereof one cannot speak," said Ludwig Wittgenstein, "thereof one must remain silent." Surely he was thinking of the poetic. The poetic cannot really be spoken 'about' but only in its own terms. The poetic has everything to do with knowledge. Let us say that it is a particular kind of knowledge. Like all knowledge, however, the poetic must be manifest in some tangible, perceptible way. Unlike most knowledge, however, this tangibility exists only in an absence, absence here understood not as nothingness, but as the space of something which exists, but is missing.

Arthur Schopenhauer said that beauty is the knowledge we gain from pleasure, whereas the sublime (which is closer to 'the poetic' in our sense here) is the knowledge we gain from suffering. It is, in other words, a particularly important knowledge implicit in everything around us, but which can never be explicitly present. There is no doubt that we experience the knowledge of this crucial absence as a deep kind of suffering.

However, Jean-François Lyotard has said, "It is clear that it is not our business to supply reality but to invent allusions to the conceivable which cannot be presented." He chooses to face forthrightly the task at hand, "inventing allusions to the conceivable." The absent knowledge can be alluded to, if not presented. It can, in short, be realized through evocation.

The evocation of the absent, through allusion, suggestion, through the making felt as sharply as possible the absence itself, is the first and most important task of art.

What, then, is this knowledge of something which is implicit in everything around us and yet which cannot be presented, therefore is always missing? Let us say that it is the knowledge of *the whole*.

We experience the world only in fragments and yet, the unfolding of time, the experience of growth and decay, the many similarities between our experiences and those of others, and even the differences in these experiences imply an order inherent in all things and events. We sense this order most especially in the organic unity of our physiological and mental processes, in the very thoughts of 'a whole' to which all the fragments must, we believe, belong. These thoughts are the origin of our personal authenticity, and thus of our need to innovate, to invent our own existences out of the fragmentary substance of our experiences of the world.

It has been said that every artist creates a world. What this statement means is that every artist worthy of the name *evokes* a world, because a world, a whole, cannot be literally created, made present, without itself becoming a fragment.

Only the innovation inherent in a work of art evokes "the conceivable which cannot be presented." And innovation occurs only when the artist takes a special kind of risk. This is the risk of working and living in the paradoxical, in the intense materiality of what is present that creates in us an experience of what is not. It is the risk of understanding the potential of the human to be human, without ever fully realizing it. This is the risk of the poetic, and the very crisis of innovation.

---

[1] "Entertainment and bread" were what Roman tyrants like Diocletian believed were sufficient to pacify the masses, and make them easy to rule.

[2] See the author's article, "Utopia Unbound: Russian and Soviet Avant-Garde, 1915-32," A+U (Architecture and Urbanism), Tokyo, February 1993, pp. 4-11. A discussion of the relationship between art and power.

[3] Said in response to a question posed by the author, during a colloquium held at the Urban Center in midtown Manhattan, March, 1994.

[4] Rem Koolhaas, S,M,L,XL, Monacelli Press, 1995, p. xix.

[5] Written for the seminar course given by the author entitled "Ethics of the Poetic" given with fifth year students at the Irwin S. Chanin School of Architecture of The Cooper Union, New York City, in February 1997

Daniel Libeskind

Traces of the Unborn

For some time now I have been working on a project I have termed the "Traces of the Unborn" — a term describing the need to resist the erasure of history, the need to respond to history, the need to open the future: that is, to delineate the invisible on the basis of the visible. Out of this meditation I have developed certain planning and architectural concepts which reflect my interest and commitment to the memory of the city; to the time in which it dwells; and to the freedom it represents.

Even if anywhere-becoming-somewhere arrives, the age of the closure of sites might yet bid farewell to *genius loci*, that idol of politics, the ultimate onto-theological component of Architecture Appropriated.

The consideration of these issues with respect to the future development of the contemporary city raises fundamental questions concerning damage to urban fabrics past, present and future, whether this damage is caused by war, economic conditions, or political ideology. Faced with these conditions, contemporary urbanism must leave aside conventional forms of contextualism and utopianism in favour of strategies enabling the transformation and metamorphosis of existing realities which take the discontinuity of the city as a positive point of departure for the construction of new urban perspectives.

The *genius loci* is but a realm invested with twenty centuries of metaphysical oppression masking the impotence of ecumenic empires to control places and the human addiction to the orientation of space.

There is an important need in every society to identify the icons which constitute a particular area, the structures which form the texture of living memory. In refuting the past and the future alike, the eternal present of transformation and metamorphosis must be incorporated in an urban framework which encourages the creation of unpredictable, flexible and hybrid architectures. At the same time the given should not be treated as an obstacle or as a form of pathology, but rather as an opportunity pregnant with new relations and urban experiences.

The implications for the city and Architecture which follow from the de-theoretization of somewhere are constructively exhilarating.

It is necessary for contemporary architects and planners to challenge the whole notion of the Masterplan with its implied finality; its misguided ambition of eternal recurrence of the same through replication. Rather, they must develop open and ever changeable methodologies which reinforce the processes of transformation and articulate the dynamic of change in a diverse and pluralistic architecture. They must both trace and steer through time and space the course of the city; the city as both a

Jewish Museum, Berlin. Photographs by Lotte Elkiaer

memory and a dream; as the House of Being and the Matrix of Hope.

The line of incision cutting the mind is straight and long — slice manipulating dearth.

Following Paul Valéry's axiom that "humanity is permanently threatened by two dangers: order and disorder," my own search for a new and responsive urbanism navigates between the Scylla of nostalgic historicism and the Charybdis of totalitarian *tabula rasa*. In doing so, it rejects both simulation in the service of respectful modesty, and destruction in the service of ideological purity. It is the search for a process which seeks to define the often invisible meanings embodied in the misunderstood, discarded, transient or forgotten typologies and situations which make up the specific energy of the city. It addresses the city's complex history as a heterogeneous spatial and temporal network, whose connections and contradictions form the basis for critical modes for intervention.

Is there a site somewhere, which does not commemorate the 'turn' of history toward its own presence, while anticipating someone else's absence?

The resulting structures suggest a new connection or knot between urban areas and their surroundings, between buildings and their sites, interacting with existing conditions by both supplementing and subverting networks of traffic, street pattern, building and open space. They are open, flexible matrices, out of which can emerge forms of architecture and urban space whose expression and representation are indistinguishable from the political space they occupy. This matrix represents a histogram of invisible realities and their relations, a graph in time and space describing the equation of a city's soul.

Is there a place anywhere — even somewhere out of this world — which does not claim to be the focal point for the transport of Being, a Being always disappearing in a post-mortem of the future?

The city is the greatest spiritual creation of humanity; a collective work which develops the expression of culture, society, and the individual in time and space. Its structure is intrinsically mysterious, developing more like a dream than a piece of equipment. Given this, alternatives are required to traditional urban planning ideas, which imply continuity based on projection. My own project in search of the contemporary city represents one possible alternative — an approach which understands and celebrates the city as an evolving, poetic and unpredictable event.

This essay is extracted from Libeskind Speaks – Writing of Construction *(Papadakis, 1998)*

THE END OF PLACE?

Dimitri A. Fatouros

If architecture is the art of the creation of *place* where does that leave the question of the end of architecture?

If architecture is just an "object" indifferent to the human condition, asking only for the incorporation of effervescent impressions into urban scenarios or open-air landscapes, then even when it pretends to represent place, if it is gigantic or not to scale, it will always be both aggressive and cynical with respect to the poetic quality of the human habitat. But it seems that such "objects" will not cease to exist.

It is this kind of "object" that is offered by the main trends of architecture today. Their number seems to open an era of monopolization of the environment. They accept and absorb any transformation and any combination of technology and subordinate architecture to an exercise in media-technology and propositions for so-called new needs and uses. The *uncritical* use of such technological propositions pays no heed to how and where they are applied.

Such "objects" transform promenades and sequences of body movement into transfer corridors and mass transportation links. The serenity of the protective cell and the shadows of glorious porticoes are transformed into calculated constructions that obey either facile mechanistic statistics or expressionistic graphics.

If architecture is the creation of *place* or *locus* or *topos*, meaning the creation of physical and symbolic situations for the understanding and contemplation of the human condition, then the question takes on a different hue.

In this case, the environment projected by these "objects," offers situations and relationships that include creative interaction, respect for one another, sympathetic living space, the sensual attractiveness of shadows, and a sense of serenity and passion for the quietness of the cell. In this way, they serve to create an environment of quality and at the same time to ensure a related way of life that represents the whole scope of the creation of place.

It is interesting to note that the supporters of these "objects" with sarcastic cynicism define as minimal an expression of any creation of place that does not accept their "objects." And so the desire for a non-gigantic and non-"noisy" environment is considered only as a low-profile expression of their work.

Instead of lively co-habitation with new everyday facilities that make full use of all that new technologies with their magical possibilities can add to the quality of life and to the qualities of place, the new facilities are used only for their show and ostentation.

Instead of creative coexistence between human beings, what is on offer today is degeneration and forced isolation. Isolated individuals perform as components of various super-competitive entities, instead of trying to cultivate togetherness and the qualities of the person.

If this is the case, at least in the more publicized trends of today's architecture, then the place that architecture should create is endangered, perhaps even lost.

Within this frame, despite the deterministic and futurological flavour of the question, we may objectively ask if this is the end of the *city*. The end of the city may signify the establishment of the mechanically assembled elements of agglomerations and the accumulation of perishable and insecure individuals. In other words, the question is whether the members of the community of the city, the *citizens*, may be facing their end.

Following this line of thought, the discussion about the end of architecture may lead to questions concerning the heart of the existence of the human condition.

One way out of this situation may be to re-introduce *nature* into the man-made environment, not as a large garden or as a landscaping technique, but as a way of life. In other words, to understand nature as a criterion for the relationship of man with the environment as expressed in the habitat. If it follows this direction, architecture can create places where fascinating new technologies are introduced and where learning from nature and coexisting with nature provide creative possibilities for human life.

In more objective terms, the question may be defined as follows: whether or not this is the end of architecture, or the *existence* or not of *architecture*, is in essence a question of the *existence* of *human* culture.

THE ARCHITECTURE OF CLOUDS

Prix. Swiczinsky. Himmelb(l)au.

The city is like a field of clouds. The rubber grid of a networked city.

The builders of the Tower of Babel were missing the material reinforced concrete. We are missing the material of the confusion of languages which we need to complete it.

There is no solution for the city.
The strategies of urban planning operate on the matrix of diverging impossibilities.
The architect has to choose one and claim responsibility for it.

Clouds are symbols for conditions that change quickly. They form and transform themselves through the complex interaction of changing situations. Viewed in slow motion, the architecture of urban development could be compared with patches of clouds.

The vocabulary of urban planning should be in an architectural antique shop and replaced by phantasms still to be defined, which fluctuate and flicker like the television screen after a broadcast.
The white noise of urban strategy, as a digitally networked system without hierarchy, is the play of suburb and periphery which will mould and determine the image of our cities and the quality they have to offer.

The notions of centre, axis and spatial sequence will have to be replaced by tangent, vector and sequence of images. We should not regret the loss of public space, but reinterpret it as a fluctuating, networked mediated event. One which acts more like a semi-conductor than a sequence of spaces.

The development of architecture is also furthered by strategies which are compromised by searching for lines and fields of possibilities tied together by chance, anti-logic and anti-authority.
But the coincidence of systems – both as built space and as media space – becomes the basis for new designs and projects, the rubber grid as the premonition of a dynamic design-net for cities like clouds.

THE END OF SCIENCE
Facing the Limits of Knowledge in the Twilight of the Scientific Age
by John Horgan

John Horgan is a one of the best science journalists and senior writer at *Scientific American*. He builds on his experience of meeting the world's leading scientists such as Richard Dawkins, Murray Gell-Mann, Stephen Hawking, Stephen Jay Gould, Roger Penrose and E.O. Wilson to examine the possibility that pure science is coming to an end. He has the ability to present complex problems accessibly and, what is more, succeeds in doing so in an entertaining way. Horgan points out that modern scientists, like Harold Bloom's poets, are latecomers. "Scientists must endure not merely Shakespeare's *King Lear*, but Newton's law of motion, Darwin's theory of natural selection, and Einstein's theory of general relativity. These theories are not merely beautiful; they are also true, empirically true." The extracts that follow are on themes with which architecture has more than a passing acquaintance. We are grateful to the author and to Little, Brown and Company for permission to reproduce them.

A star-forming dark cloud imaged by Isocam. The scattered bright dots are new stars of moderate size, comparable in mass to the Sun. The bright fuzzy object is a new massive star, much heavier than the Sun, still wrapped in the placental cloud from which it formed. Photo: ESA/ISO, CEA Saclay and ISOCAM Consortium

John Horgan

The End of Chaoplexity

The field of chaoplexity emerged as a full-blown pop-culture phenomenon with the publication in 1987 of Chaos: Making a New Science, *by James Gleick. Horgan says that by chaoplexity he means "both chaos and its close relative complexity. Each term, and chaos in particular, has been defined in specific, distinct ways by specific individuals. But each has also been defined in so many overlapping ways by so many different scientists and journalists that the terms have become virtually synonymous, if not meaningless."*

There are two, somewhat contradictory aspects to the chaoplexity message. One is that many phenomena are nonlinear and hence inherently unpredictable, because arbitrarily tiny influences can have enormous, unforeseeable consequences. Edward Lorenz, a meteorologist at MIT and a pioneer of chaoplexity, called this phenomenon the butterfly effect, because it meant that a butterfly fluttering in Iowa could, in principle, trigger an avalanche of effects culminating in a monsoon in Indonesia. Because we can never possess more than approximate knowledge of a weather system, our ability to predict its behaviour is severely limited.

This insight is hardly new. Henri Poincaré warned at the turn of the century that "small differences in the initial conditions produce very great ones in the final phenomena. A small error in the former will produce an enormous error in the latter. Prediction becomes impossible."[1] Investigators of chaoplexity – whom I will call chaoplexologists – also like to emphasize that many phenomena in nature are "emergent;" they exhibit properties that cannot be predicted or understood simply by examining the system's parts. Emergence, too, is a hoary idea, related to holism, vitalism, and other antireductionist creeds that date back to the last century at least. Certainly Darwin did not think that natural selection could be derived from Newtonian mechanics.

So much for the negative side of the chaoplexity message. The positive side goes as follows: the advent of computers and of sophisticated nonlinear mathematical techniques will help modern scientists understand chaotic, complex, emer-gent phenomena that have resisted analysis by the reductionist methods of the past. The blurb on the back of Heinz Pagels's *The Dreams of Reason*, one of the best books on the "new sciences of complexity," put it this way: "Just as the telescope opened up the universe and the microscope revealed the secrets of the microcosm, the computer is now opening an exciting new window on the nature of reality. Through its capacity to process what is too complex for the unaided mind, the computer enables us for the first time to simulate reality, to create models of complex systems like large molecules, chaotic systems, neural nets, the human body and brain, and patterns of evolution and population growth."[2]

This hope stems in large part from the observation that simple sets of mathematical instructions, when carried out by a computer, can yield fantastically complicated and yet strangely ordered effects. John von Neumann may have been the first scientist to recognize this capability of computers. In the 1950s, he invented the cellular automaton, which in its simplest form is a screen divided into a grid of cells, or squares. A set of rules relates the colour, or state, of each cell to the state of its immediate neighbours. A change in the state of a single cell can trigger a cascade of changes throughout the entire system. "Life," created in the early 1970s by the British mathematician John Conway, remains one of the most cel-ebrated of cellular automatons. Whereas most cellular au-tomatons eventually settle into predictable, periodic behav-iour, Life generates an infinite variety of patterns – including cartoonlike objects that seem to be engaged in inscruta-ble missions. Inspired by Conway's strange computer world, a number of scientists began using cellular automatons to model various physical and biological processes.

Another product of computer science that seized the im-agination of the scientific community was the Mandelbrot set. The set is named after Benoit Mandelbrot, an applied mathematician at IBM who is one of the protagonists of Gleick's book *Chaos* (and whose work on indeterministic phenomena led Gunther Stent to conclude that the social sciences would never amount to much). Mandelbrot invented fractals, mathematical objects displaying what is known as fractional dimensionality: they are fuzzier than a line but never quite fill a plane. Fractals also display patterns that keep recurring at finer and finer scales. After coining the term fractal, Mandelbrot pointed out that many real-world phenomena – notably clouds, snowflakes, coastlines, stockmarket fluctuations, and trees – have fractal-like properties.

The Mandelbrot set, too, is a fractal. The set corresponds to a simple mathematical function that is repeatedly iterated; one solves the function and plugs the answer back into it and solves it again, ad infinitum. When plotted by a computer, the numbers generated by the function cluster into a now-famous shape, which has been likened to a tumour-ridden heart, a badly burned chicken, and a warty figure eight lying on its side. When one magnifies the set with a computer, one finds that its borders do not form crisp lines, but shimmer like flames. Repeated magnification of the borders plunges the viewer into a bottomless phantasmagoria of baroque imagery. Certain patterns, such as the basic heartlike shape, keep recurring, but always with subtle variations.

The Mandelbrot set, which has been called "the most complex object in mathematics," has become a kind of laboratory in which mathematicians can test ideas about the behaviour of nonlinear (or chaotic, or complex) systems. But what relevance do those findings have to the real world? In his 1977 magnum opus, *The Fractal Geometry of Nature*, Mandelbrot warned that it was one thing to observe a fractal pattern in nature and quite another to determine the *cause* of that pattern. Although exploring the consequences of self-similarity yielded "extraordinary surprises, helping me to understand the fabric of nature," Mandelbrot said, his attempts to unravel the causes of self-similarity "had few charms."[3] Mandelbrot seemed to be alluding to the seductive syllogism that underlies chaoplexity. The syllogism is this: There are simple sets of mathematical rules that when followed by a computer give rise to extremely complicated patterns, patterns that never quite repeat themselves. The natural world also contains many extremely complicated patterns that never quite repeat themselves. Conclusion: Simple rules underlie many extremely complicated phenomena in the world. With the help of powerful computers, chaoplexologists can root out those rules.

Of course, simple rules do underlie nature, rules embodied in quantum mechanics, general relativity, natural selection, and Mendelian genetics. But chaoplexologists insist that much more powerful rules remain to be found.

Cybernetics and Other Catastrophes
History abounds with failed attempts to create a mathematical theory that explains and predicts a broad range of phenomena, including social ones. In the seventeenth century Leibniz fantasized about a system of logic so compelling that it could resolve not only all mathematical questions but also philosophical, moral, and political ones.[4] Leibniz's dream has persisted even in the century of doubt. Since World War II scientists have become temporarily infatuated with at least three such theories: cybernetics, information theory, and catastrophe theory.

Cybernetics was created largely by one person, Norbert Wiener, a mathematician at the Massachusetts Institute of Technology. The subtitle of his 1948 book, *Cybernetics*, revealed his ambition: *Control and Communication in the Animal and the Machine*.[5] Wiener based his neologism on the Greek term *kubernetes*, or steersman. He proclaimed that it should be possible to create a single, overarching theory that could explain the operation not only of machines but also of all biological phenomena, from single-celled organisms up through the economies of nation-states. All these entities process and act on information; they all employ such mechanisms as positive and negative feedback and filters to distinguish signals from noise.

By the 1960s cybernetics had lost its lustre. The eminent electrical engineer John R. Pierce noted dryly in 1961 that "in this country the word cybernetics has been used most extensively in the press and in popular and semiliterary, if not semiliterate, magazines."[6] Cybernetics still has a following in isolated enclaves, notably Russia (which during the Soviet era was highly receptive to the fantasy of society as a machine that could be fine-tuned by following the precepts of cybernetics). Wiener's influence persists in U.S. pop culture if not within science itself: we owe words such as *cyberspace*, *cyberpunk*, and *cyborg* to Wiener.

Closely related to cybernetics is information theory, which Claude Shannon, a mathematician at Beel Laboratories, spawned in 1948 with a two-part paper titled "A Mathematical Theory of Communication."[7] Shannon's great achievement was to invent a mathematical definition of information based on the concept of entropy in thermodynamics. Unlike cybernetics, information theory continues to thrive – within the niche for which it was intended. Shannon's theory was designed to improve the transmission of information over a telephone or telegraph line subject to electrical interference, or noise. The theory still serves as the theoretical foundation for coding, compression, encryption, and other aspects of information processing.

By the 1960s information theory had infected other disciplines outside communications, including, linguistics, psychology, economics, biology, and even the arts. (For example, various sages tried to concoct formulas relating the quality of music to its information content.) Although information theory is enjoying a renaissance in physics as a result of the influence of Hohn Wheeler (the it from bit) and others, it has yet to contribute to physics in any concrete way. Shannon himself doubted whether certain applications of his theory would come to much. "Somehow people think it can tell you things about meaning," he once said to me, "but it can't and wasn't intended to."[8]

Perhaps the most oversold metatheory was the appropriately named catastrophe theory, invented by the French mathematician René Thom in the 1960s. Thom developed the theory as a purely mathematical formalism, but he and others began to claim that it could provide insights into a broad range of phenomena that displayed discontinuous behaviour. Thom's magnum opus was his 1972 book, *Structural Stability and Morphogenesis*, which received awestruck reviews in Europe and the United States. A reviewer in the *Times* of

London declared that "it is impossible to give a brief description of the impact of this book. In one sense the only book with which it can be compared in Newton's *Principia*. Both lay out a new conceptual framework for the understanding of nature, and equally both go on to unbounded speculation."[9]

Thom's equations revealed how a seemingly ordered system could undergo abrupt, "catastrophic" shifts from one state to another. Thom and his followers suggested that these equations could help to explain not only such purely physical events as earthquakes, but also biological and social phenomena, such as the emergence of life, the metamorphosis of a caterpillar into a butterfly, and the collapse of civilizations. By the late 1970s, the counterattack had begun. Two mathematicians declared in *Nature* that catastrophe theory "is one of many attempts to deduce the world by thought alone." They called that "an appealing dream, but a dream that cannot come true." Other critics charged that Thom's work "provides no new information about anything" and is "exaggerated, not wholly honest."[10]

Chaos, as defined by James Yorke, exhibited this same boom-bust. By 1991, at least one pioneer of chaos theory, the French mathematician David Ruelle, had begun to wonder whether his field had passed its peak. Ruelle invented the concept of strange attractors, mathematical objects that have fractal properties and can be used to describe the behaviour of systems that never settle into a periodic pattern. In his book *Chance and Chaos*, Ruelle noted that chaos "has been invaded by swarms of people who are attracted by success, rather than the ideas involved. And this changes the intellectual atmosphere for the worse. ... The physics of chaos, in spite of frequent triumphant announcements of 'novel' breakthroughs, has had a declining output of interesting discoveries. Hopefully, when the craze is over, a sober appraisal of the difficulties of the subject will result in a new wave of high-quality results."[11]

The Poetry of Artificial Life

Christopher Langton [the founding father of artificial life] complained that he was frustrated with the linearity of scientific language. "There's a reason for poetry," he said. "Poetry is a very nonlinear use of language, where the meaning is more than just the sum of the parts. And science requires that it be nothing more than the sum of the parts. And just the fact that there's stuff to explain out there that's more than the sum of the parts means that the traditional approach, just characterizing the parts and the relations, is not going to be adequate for capturing the essence of many systems that you would like to be able to do. That's not to say that there isn't a way to do it in a more scientific way than poetry, but I just have the feeling that culturally there's going to be more of something like poetry in the future of science."

Making Metaphors

The fields of chaos [and] complexity ... will continue. Certain practitioners will be content to play in the realm of pure mathematics and theoretical computer science. Others, the majority, will develop new mathematical and computational techniques for engineering purposes. They will make incremental advances, such as extending the range of weather forecasts or improving the ability of engineers to simulate the performance of jets or other complex technologies. But they will not achieve any great insights into nature – certainly none comparable to Darwin's theory of evolution or quantum mechanics. They will not force any significant revisions in our map of reality or our narrative of creation. ...

So far, chaoplexologists have created some potent metaphors: the butterfly effect, fractals, artificial life, the edge of chaos, self-organized criticality. But they have not told us anything about the world that is both concrete and truly surprising, either in a negative or positive sense. They have slightly extended the borders of knowledge in certain areas, and more sharply delineated the boundaries of knowledge elsewhere. Computer simulations represent a kind of metareality within which we can play with and even – to a limited degree – test scientific theories, but they are not reality itself (although many aficionados have lost sight of that distinction). Moreover, by giving scientists more power to manipulate different symbols in different ways to simulate a natural phenomenon, computers may undermine scientists' faith that their theories are not only true but *True*, exclusively and absolutely true. Computers may, if anything, hasten the end of empirical science. Christopher Langton was right: there is something more like poetry in the future of science.

1. Gleick printed this quote from Poincaré in *Chaos*, p. 321.
2. *The Dreams of Reason*, Heinz Pagels, Simon and Schuster, New York, 1988. The blurb quoted is on the July 1989 paperback edition by Bantam.
3. *The Fractal Geometry of Nature*, Benoit Mandelbrot, W.H. Freeman, San Francisco, 1977, p. 423. The remark earlier in the paragraph that the Mandelbrot set is "the most complex object in mathematics" was made by the computer scientist A.K. Dewdney in *Scientific American*, August 1985, p. 16.
4. A discussion of Leibniz's belief in an "irrefutable calculus" that could solve all problems, even theological ones, can be found in the excellent book *Pi in the Sky*, by John Barrow, Oxford University Press, New York, 1992, pp. 127–129.
5. *Cybernetics*, by Norbert Wiener, was published in 1948 by John Wiley and Sons, New York.
6. John R. Pierce made this comment about cybernetics on page 210 of his book *An Introduction to Information Theory*, Dover, New York, 1980 (originally published in 1961).
7. Claude Shannon's paper, "A Mathematical Theory of Communications," was published in the *Bell System Technical Journal*, July and October, 1948.
8. Interview with Shannon at his home in Winchester, Mass., in November 1989. The author also wrote a profile of him for *Scientific American*, January 1990, pp. 22-22b.
9. This glowing review of Thom's book appeared in the *London Times Higher Education Supplement*, November 30, 1973. Horgan found the reference in *Searching for Certainty*, by John Casti, William Morrow, New York, 1990, pp. 63-64. Casti, who has written a number of excellent books on mathematics-related topics, is associated with the Santa Fe Institute. The English translation of Thom's book *Structural Stability and Morphogenesis*, originally issued in French in 1972, was published in 1975 by Addison-Wesley, Reading, Mass.
10. These negative comments about catastrophe theory were reprinted in Casti, *Searching for Certainty*, p. 417.
11. *Chance and Chaos*, David Ruelle, Princeton University Press, Princeton, N.J., 1991, p. 72. This book is a quiet but profound meditation on the meaning of chaos by one of its pioneers.

THE END OF ORDER
The Tanner Foundation Lectures delivered at Brasenose College, Oxford
by Francis Fukuyama

It is almost a decade since the publication of Francis
Fukuyama's first article, soon to be followed by a most
interesting book, on the end of history,
implying the end of culture as we know it.
It was at the origin of the flurry of 'End ofs' on the
bookshelves and brought to the surface
deep doubts about the endless reservoir of
man's intellectual achievements.
Fukuyama suggested that what had come to an end
was not the occurrence of events but history understood
as a single, coherent evolutionary process.
Despite the existence of injustice and serious
social problems in today's liberal democracies,
the *ideal* of liberal democracy could not be improved on
and may constitute the "end point of mankind's ideological
evolution," the "final form of human government,"
and thus the "end of history."
His recent series of lectures on *The End of Order* and their
publication by the influential Social Market Foundation are a
welcome addition to the series.
Born in Japan but brought up in New York, Fukuyama was
deputy director at the US State Department's Policy Planning
department. He is now Professor of Public Policy and
director of the Centre for Global Political Economy
at George Mason University in Virginia. He is presently
working on *The Great Disruption to be published next year*.
We are grateful to the author and to the Social Market Foundation for permission to reproduce the following extracts.

Francis Fukuyama

The End of Order

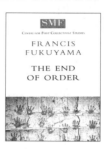

In The End of Order *Fukuyama's contention is that the undermining of the family and marriage is central to social breakdown and that the primary engine for generating the social capital which societies need to function properly is increasingly under strain. He claims that a combination of oral contraception and greater female participation in the labour market has led to what he calls 'the Great Disruption,' a period of social upheaval not seen since the industrial revolution. The raison d'être for marriage has collapsed. Men no longer feel constrained to limit their fertility to the women and children they can support economically. Women can no longer rely on men and are increasingly supporting themselves and their offspring independently or through the state instead. The result is that an entire generation is growing up without fathers to socialize them, a generation which is more prone to educational failure, violence and criminality than its predecessors. Fukuyama says that new ways must be found of producing the social capital which is the buttress against social breakdown.*

Social Capital

An extraordinary amount of attention has been paid to the interrelated issues of social capital, civil society, trust and social norms as central issues for contemporary democracies. ... Social capital is an important and relatively under-studied factor in explaining certain characteristics of the global economy.[1]

In contrast to the related concept of human capital, there is less consensus today about what social capital is, how it can be measured, where it comes from and particularly how to get more of it.

Social capital: definitions

The first use of the term 'social capital' that I am aware of was in Jane Jacob's classic *The Death and Life of Great American Cities* (1961), in which she explained that the dense social networks in older-mixed-use urban neighbourhoods constituted a form of social capital, and was far more responsible for cleanliness, absence of street crime and other quality-of-life measures than were formal institutional factors like police protection.[2] ...

Social capital can be defined simply as the existence of a certain set of informal values or norms shared among members of a group that permit co-operation among them. The sharing of values and norms does not in itself produce social capital, because the values may be the wrong ones. ...

The Mafia is characterized by an extremely strong internal code of behaviour, *l'omerta*, and individual mafiosi are spoken of as 'men of honour.' Nevertheless, these norms do not apply outside a small circle of mafiosi; for the rest of Sicilian society, the prevailing norms can be described more as 'take advantage of people outside your immediate family at every occasion otherwise they will take advantage of you first.' Obviously, such norms do not promote social cooperation and the negative consequences for both government and economic development have been extensively documented.[3]

The norms that produce social capital, by contrast, must substantively include virtues like truth-telling, the meeting of obligations and reciprocity. Not surprisingly, these norms overlap to a significant degree with the Puritan values ... critical to the development of Western capitalism.

It is clear that the norms that produce social capital are partible, that is, they can only be shared among limited groups of people, not among others in the same society. While social capital exists in all societies, it can be distributed in very different ways. Families are obviously universally important sources. But the family structure differs from one society to another and the strength of family bonds differs, not simply from family ties in other societies, but relative to other types of social tie. In some cases, there appears to be something of an inverse relationship between the bonds of trust and reciprocity within kinship groups and between kin and non-kin; while one is very strong, the other is very weak. What made the Reformation important for Weber was not so much that it encouraged honesty, reciprocity and thrift among individuals but that these virtues were for the first time widely practised outside the family.[4]

It is perfectly possible to form successful groups in the absence of social capital, using a variety of formal coordination mechanisms like contracts, hierarchies, constitutions, legal systems and the like. But informal norms greatly reduce the transaction costs entailed by these mechanisms, and under certain circumstances may facilitate a higher degree of group adaptation. Civil society, which has been the focus of considerable democratic theorizing in recent years, is in large measure the product of social capital, though in certain important respects not completely congruent with it.

There are two points that need to be made about social capital. First of all, it is not a subset of human capital because it is a property of groups and not individuals. Conventional human capital — education and skills — can be acquired by Robinson Crusoe on his proverbial desert island. The norms underlying social capital, by contrast, must be shared by more than one individual to have any meaning. The group endowed with social capital may be as small as two friends who share information or collaborate on a common project or it can be as large as an entire nation.

Second, social capital is not necessarily a good thing, with regard to either politics or economics. Co-ordination is necessary for all social activity, whether good or bad. Socrates, responding to Thrasymachos' contention that justice was merely the advantage of the stronger, notes in Book I of the Republic that even a band of robbers must have a sense of justice among themselves, or else they could not succeed in pulling off their robberies. The Mafia and the Ku Klux Klan, for example, are both social groups who are violent and murder but who are nonetheless constituent parts of American civil society. In economic life, group co-ordination is necessary for a form of production, but when technology or markets change, a different type of co-ordination with perhaps a different set of group members becomes necessary. Bonds of social reciprocity that facilitated production in the earlier time period become obstacles to production later. To continue the economic metaphor, social capital to that point can be said to be obsolete and needs to be depreciated in the society's capital accounts.

Social capital and the broader problem of modernity

The debate over American social capital reflects a much broader and more important question: whether, as economic development progresses, we are witnessing an unravelling of the larger Enlightenment project of building a modern world order based on the rule of reason. The modern liberal project envisioned replacing a community based on tradition, religion, race or culture with one based on a formal social contract among rational individuals who come together to preserve their natural rights as human beings. Rather than seeking the moral improvement of their members, modern societies have sought to create institutions like constitutional government and market-based exchange to regulate individual behaviour.

From the earliest days of the Enlightenment, conservative thinkers like Burke and de Maistre argued that such a community could not work. Without the transcendental sanctions posed by religion, without the irrational attachments, loyalties and duties born out of culture and historical tradition, modern societies would come apart at the seams.

Other thinkers less hostile to the Enlightenment have nonetheless recognized the importance of moral norms in the functioning of modern liberal democracy. Most important was Tocqueville, who wrote extensively on the kinds of moral habits and customs necessary to sustain a system of limited government. It was Tocqueville, of course, who pointed to the American 'art of association' as underpinning the dense and complex civil society in the United States; an art that served as a school for democratic self-government and permitted the self-organization of large sectors of American society.

It has long been recognized that economic modernization brings in its wake changes in fundamental values and norms; indeed, the entire discipline of sociology has been described as one long commentary on the shift from Gemeinschaft to Gesellschaft. In the heyday of 'modernization theory' in the 1950s and early 1960s, this value shift — from traditional to modern, from ascriptive to voluntary, from status to achievement — was largely regarded as a difficult but positive and necessary transition societies had to go through before they stabilized around the tidy norms of contemporary suburban America. The problem was that values did not stop evolving and the shift towards a post-industrial society that gathered steam in the 1960s seemed to be accompanied by a new set of norms — particularly the deterioration of the nuclear family and a rise in various forms of social deviance — that were not so obviously healthy.

One consequence is that earlier arguments about the self-undermining character of the Enlightenment have been revived by a number of thinkers in recent years. John Gray, for example has argued that the social deterioration apparent in contemporary America marks the inevitable disintegration of the Enlightenment experiment.[5] Modern societies based on Enlightenment principles – constitutional democracy in the political sphere and the capitalist market – have succeeded, according to this line of thought, only because they have been able to live off several centuries of accumulated social capital. That is, the social constraints formerly provided by religion and other non-creating cultural institutions have survived into the current secular age only out of a kind of reflexive habit, but such societies are ultimately unable to generate new social capital.

Fears that the stock of social capital is being deleted are not new, they were around during the late nineteenth century transitions from agrarian to industrial societies in Europe and north America. Social capital had new and unexpected sources in these industrial societies. It is useful to revisit some of the broader questions of macrosociology raised at that time, for at least two reasons. First, since the great classics of sociology describing the earlier transition were written, there as been another massive shift in social norms and, I would argue, decline in older forms of social capital for which some account needs to be given. Second, we now have data on a number of non-Western modernized societies – primarily in Asia – that will serve as useful points of comparison in trying to understand whether these shifts in norms are the product of modernization per se, or rather the particular path modernization has taken in the West.

The Great Disruption
Social norms have been subject to continuous change throughout human history, and for the societies that have experienced industrialization and economic modernization, the rate of change has moved to higher levels since these processes began.

That being said, it is striking how rapidly norms have shifted throughout the industrialized world in the three decades between approximately 1965 and 1995. The rate of change in a variety of social indicators has been so great that this entire period deserves to be characterized as a 'Great Disruption' in earlier patterns of social life.

The primary change that has occurred has been a decline of the nuclear family. ... There is substantial evidence that this decline is linked causally to a whole series of changes in social norms and outcomes, including crime, child abuse, poverty, educational achievement. ... The reasons why this decline occurred are, needless to say, complex, and arise out of the interaction of certain economic and technological changes and social norms and values.

Explanations for the 'Great Disruption'
The changes in social norms that I have labelled the Great Disruption have been massive in their cumulative scope, rapid and spread over a very wide range of countries.
Large social phenomena of this sort generally have a variety of interrelated causes, and observers have attributed these changes to factors such as poverty and economic disruption, shifts in cultural values, feminism and the movement of women into the labour force, government policy, including levels and types of welfare benefits, changing technology, television and other forms of mass communication, inherent defects in liberal ideology, the decline of religion and the like.

Social capital and post-industrial society
Despite the collapse of Communism and the evident failure of virtually all serious competitors to the liberal-democratic Enlightenment order, the verdict is still not in. As the industrial period gives way to the post-industrial era, and as information and services become the chief sources of new wealth in the economy, informal social norms play a renewed role in innovation and production. The collapse of Taylorite scientific management signals the limits of organization founded solely on rule-based bureaucratic rationalism; its replacement by flat or networked forms of management and self-organization signal the continuing requirement for informal norm-based co-ordination. And to some extent, the increasing demand for such norm-based organization is calling forth a corresponding supply... There are some sectors of American society that probably have higher levels of social capital than in previous historical periods.

On the other hand, economic change has made the Great Disruption possible, which in turn has undermined certain critical co-operative norms related to the family and spawned a host of related social pathologies. It is not clear that we are moving spontaneously toward the creation of a new set of norms regarding, for example, gender relations, that will serve as a socially-optimal substitute with regard to such functions as the socialization of children. Under these circumstances, the state has intervened to mitigate the consequences of these shifting norms, usually with less than optimal results and at increasingly great economic cost. The current crisis of the welfare state is this: even if it were affordable it is not clear that the state can adequately perform the socialization functions traditionally played by other, smaller-scale social groups and without hastening the demise of those very groups.

If the state is finally incapable of rebuilding social capital, the question is whether it will come from other sources. My earlier taxonomy of norm-generation suggests that apart from rational institutional sources, norms can be generated spontaneously through the repeated interactions of individual agents, or exogenously through the introduction of a new set of moral norms. ... The question is how long this evolution will take, what mechanisms might intervene to speed up the process and how much damage will be done in the meantime. ...

We can draw some comfort by looking at other historical periods, and noting that societies have been able to regenerate social capital in the past. Historical data on social trends are necessarily sketchy, but it is clear that the levels of social deviance evident in the developed world today are not historically unprecedented. ...

The great classic figures of social theory – Marx, Tönnies, Weber, Durkheim and Simmel – need to be written anew to take account of what is easily as momentous a shift as the one they experienced during their own lives.

[1] These are the broad themes of *Trust: The Social Virtues and the Creation of Prosperity*, Free Press, New York, 1995.
[2] Jane Jacobs, *The Death and Life of Great American Cities*, Vintage Books, New York, 1961, p. 138.
[3] See, for example, Edward C. Banfield, *The Moral Basis of a Backward Society*, Free Press, Glencoe, 1958, and Robert D. Putnam, *Making Democracy Work, Civic Traditions in Modern Italy*, Princeton University Press, Princeton, 1993.
[4] According to Weber 'The great achievement of ethical religions, above all of the ethical and asceticist sects of Protestantism, was to shatter the fetters of the sib.' *The Religion of China*, Free Press, New York, 1951, p. 237.
[5] See, for example, John Gray, *Enlightenment's Wake: Politics and Culture at the Close of the Modern Age*, Routledge, London, 1995.

Francis Fukuyama

Eric Owen Moss

THE GLUE

The glue is a cerebral underground from which specific conceptual undertakings are generated. The glue is a caricatured psyche. It designates a criss-cross of emotions and ideas, piled up over many years, on which the architecture sits. The glue comes to bear in different ways, from different vantage points, at different weights, in various projects including the Samitaur project. But to say that you could actually find a particular image around a particular corner of Samitaur would be a misunderstanding. Start to disassemble the glue and it's gone. It's psychologically inviolate. Cut it into chunks to explain the mess, and the interconnections are severed. The interconnections are so fine, so precarious, so infinitesimal and so can't-be-numbered-ish, that it's not possible to break in. Nonetheless, the glue is an attempt to qualify that criss-cross. There are concerns, aspirations, apprehensions, all running together in a kind of crazy flood. I couldn't sort it out clearly. And then all of a sudden something would pop up out of the web, something would pop out and I could say, "Oh, there's a spider." And then the spider would be gone. It would be a misunderstanding to locate Chaplin or the Sistine Chapel or John Cage at Samitaur.

Over the years, as I continue to look and draw and travel and read, numerous disparate items stuck in my head. Some enter and stay for a while. Some enter and transform. Some enter and go out the other side. What the composite is, I'm never quite sure—the list and the perspective keep moving.

ABU SIMBEL

Abu Simbel on the move, making way for the Aswan Dam, contradicts the often repeated notion concerning the durability of buildings—that architecture endures. True and utterly untrue.

We don't know what we've lost. At the bottom of the sea under an avalanche, to floods and earthquakes. We guess. We surmise. We hypothesize. Perhaps whole cultures are lost. Was it really Aeschylus, Sophocles, Aristophanes and Euripedes, or are the best sitting on the bottom of the Aegean? This shrine, this colossal Egyptian construction, was cut and moved, so the waters couldn't swallow it. Where are all the pieces the waters swallowed? Abu Simbel had no site sanctity. How enduring is a site? Alter it. Manicure it. And in time become subject to being moved. Moving and being moved. Abu Simbel is majestic, maybe utterly beyond our ability to feel and to re-build. We need these connections across time that have outrun time. Progress can't run in only one direction.

AIRPLANE

When my father died, I wondered why I was combing my hair, why I was doing anything given the inevitable conclusion. But something seemed mysteriously to push me. And keeps pushing me, even when it would be logical to stop. Sisyphus. Perhaps the push comes from a continuity force. Keep going, somehow, and invent a step in order to arrive at the next step which requires the next invention. I agreed with myself to accept the possibility that I could formulate a plan, even though I couldn't say how long term the plan was.

Tatlin makes Icarus real. The dream of flight. What's great about Tatlin's glider is its innocence and enthusiasm. No ideology, no method yet, just an instinct. The pre-idol machine, the machine before **Chaplin** needed to stick his face in the gears. The machine as prospect, as experiment, not as certainty.

The technical events that first seem so astonishing, have such short lives. The taller building, the longer bridge span, the faster plane, don't appeal for long. Technical wonders lose their wonder. An ad for the movie *Airplane*. The wonder of flying isn't enough now to hold the attention of the audience. One has to twist the plane to entertain. This may account for some of the behavior in architecture today.

AJANTA

Ajanta is one of these "I'm going to have to go there" places. Whether I get there or not, it's in my head. Cave paintings of the Buddha from the second century, 800 miles north and east of Bombay. A colossal number and, apparently, remarkable in quality. Difficult to photograph. Not much light. A transcendental sensibility which makes you enormously powerful while shedding the separation that makes you *you*, distinct from other yous. The art has an appeal because of it's anonymity. The name of the artist is not important. But it is. *Because* it was left out. Which tells you a lot about the intent of the religion.

This might allow me to overcome Michelangelo's skull. It fascinates me and consoles me. There's a prospect. It's like the light coming under Kafka's Door of the Law. You can see it. You might get to it, but you might not. This is an aspiration to a crucial experience in architecture. Tension. Maybe. Maybe not. A perpetual prospect in the language of space.

ALTAMIRA

The Altamira and Lascaux cave paintings, and recent discoveries at Chauvet and Cosquier, indicate how difficult it is to master our antecedents. What trails brought us to where we are? Contributors lost? Histories buried? We don't know whether tomorrow someone's submarine will bump into Atlantis, which might explain the perplexing continuities between forms, beliefs and traditions in the Middle East and the Yucatán. Can we ever get to the bottom? To the ultimate exploration? And why do we so consistently act as if we've arrived there, only to be forced to reverse our positions? What we don't know is always much bigger than what we know.

In *The Los Angeles Times*, there was a story about the discovery of a skeleton in Spain which, according to the author, entirely re-explains the chronology of human evolution. Now, says the story, we really know what happened. No longer is it Darwin's hypothesis, but more a process of fits and starts, successes and cul-de-sacs. Arriving at current humanity was described in the story as as much a wonderful accident as a logical process.

The head of the bull in the wall painting raises the current propensity to relegate to the antiquities file material from the 60s or the 80s because: this is the 90s, of course. The ultimate in sophistication, but the 80s? How tedious and out-of-date. From this perspective almost everything that is hip is soon out of date. Then along comes Altamira with the most colossal and powerful art. These paintings are quite viable in their power and are durable and contemporary and relevant in every sense. The idea that things would get better or more sophisticated or old so quickly has to be evaluated in terms of the superficial currents of an ad agency culture. You have to keep selling, keep the goods moving. Durability stifles sales (including art sales). But deeper trends run on a different timeline.

AMAZON

Amazon River Once Flowed West. And not only that. Perhaps the change from west to east was not Darwinism, not slow, not gentle, not gradual, not over eons. Perhaps instantaneous like the asteroid hitting **Jupiter**—cataclysmic evolution. And how to bring that sensibility to architecture? **Dionysus over Apollo.** Spain over Darwin. A sensibility that suggests the world moves by jumps and fits and digressions. And if science confirms that geologically, we'll have to modify the logical, sequential perceptions of **God the Geometer.**

ANATOMY LESSON

A Rembrandt painting, *Anatomy Lesson of Dr. Tulip*—a corpse and a surgeon, explaining man to men. It all makes the same recognizable empirical sense. One part of the anatomy is attached to another. All quite logically. There is a sequence and a continuity and an order and a logic. This is in man and that empirical logic governs the entire cosmos? Not just man, but man's world. So let's celebrate the mathematics of **Pythagoras** and the logic of anatomy by placing a grid on the **Moon**. Find the logic and extend the logic. But is the logic intrinsic? Probably not. The idea that the order of things is ultimately discoverable, that it's amenable to rational scrutiny, is perhaps the vantage point of our culture at the end of the 20th century. But I detect substantial cracks in this viewpoint. Is logic an imposed veneer over a subject that continues to throw it off?

ANGKOR WAT

Angkor Wat at a pinnacle in the 10th, 9th, or 8th century, before finally giving way to the trees. Architecture is so often talked about as durable. But **it occurs to me that the most durable form of the architecture might be in print** because, almost inevitably, tenants and clients and time all kick at the building. However powerful the building, however strong its ability to withstand the kicking, however successful I have been in delivering a built experience that's powerful and man-controlled, the building is not able to withstand what ultimately rolls over everything. You don't mow the lawn—it eats the street.

I went to see the movie *The Lost World* the other day, and there was a scene where lots of tiny dinosaurs overwhelm a man. He can whack away one, two, five, ten. Ultimately, he is unrecognizable. This happens to buildings.

If you write a poem and the editor starts cutting words, punctuation, the title. You're left with pieces...like Gilgamesh. We don't have the real Gilgamesh, it's missing. Or the Dead Sea Scrolls. You have to surmise. Intriguing, but not what the author intended. Angkor Wat? Maybe the people who inhabited these colossal buildings anticipated that someday someone would come and find, not them or their progeny, but a tree growing where the King used to sit.

The tree and the King experience pushes me. I went to see *The Lost World* because I love looking at those animals. I've been like that since I was a little kid. I remember going to the Museum of Natural History in New York and looking at big skeletons of prehistoric whales. They were so powerful. What happened to all that power?

BABYLON

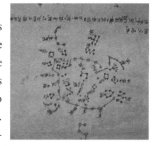

A very old drawing, a Babylonian map of the sky. It's consistent with culture's need to map. Eco's Causaubin said, "make a plan." **And a plan seems to be a cultural essential in order to account for the order of things**. If one can understand the order of things past, then presumably one can account for the present, and predict the future. Very cogent. The Babylonians had a map of the sky and, of course, it's incorrect. It leaves out lots of things. Ours do too. That's harder to take. But the tendency to continue to make maps or plans and to insist on the efficacy of those explanations seems consistent in every culture. From a distance we can see how those patterns or maps or plans have come and gone, although a suspicion of our own efforts doesn't always follow. But it should.

I recall being told in school that we knew almost everything, and just had to fill in a few details. My sense would be that we know almost nothing for a certainty, and that we can never know enough, have sufficient information to counter the inscrutable in our lives. Fundamentally, all these cultures want to say they know: how the world works, its villains, how history moves, if it does, and who's going to move it. For instance, Hegel to Marx to **Lenin** to Mao to Castro to oblivion, and the Berlin Wall is down. Or is it? Makes the taking of definitive positions on history extremely tenuous. Because you can see them disappear before your eyes. Somebody carts away the city in a truck, a tree grows out of **Angkor Wat's** foundations, Lenin sweeps out the trash, and then he himself is swept away.

BACK UP THE TRUCK

A truck backing up and hauling away the American city. Presumably intent on making room to build the next one. The return of Marinetti and Futurist hygiene. It also seems particularly applicable to Los Angeles. Building here often seems so ephemeral. The question seems to be between erasing the city and replacing

it, retaining the city quite literally and restoring it or, the in between, recollecting forward —the retention of a residual aspect of the previous pattern and incorporating it in an altered perception. A lived felt experience is sustained over time by re-evaluating priorities and symbols. Redundancy stretched over time terminates the vitality. What was once fresh becomes a repetitious method or system, finally tedious, and the light goes out.

BERKELEY

An anti-war gathering slide I shot in 1967 in Berkeley. The student movement at Berkeley against the Vietnam War and against the authority of the regents who were running the University was a great instructional process for me in human behavior. I had a chance to observe the effect of crowds on the individuals who made them up, their individual identity as a consequence of the collective identity of the crowd. I started to consider social and political allegiances, and the polarization of arguments, the caricature each side often delivers of the opposing position. The old Malcolm X line was quoted there a lot and still is—that you're either a part of the problem or a part of the solution. I had a feeling that each person actually carried both the problem and the solution within themselves. What I disliked in someone else, I often found in myself. I could never line up with one side or the other because I could see each side cartooning its position in a way that excluded the other side, but in fact there was almost always some useful truth buried in the most onerous position. The strategy seemed always to crush the opposition. In many cases I just felt I was dancing in the middle.

The related issue has to do with defining the world as numbers, as masses, as gargantuan parts. There was a constant diatribe from the left and right: "the masses" need this and "the masses" need that. **I wanted to understand life lived singly**, one person at a time. Life is personal and private, and not always exchangeable. Yacking about the interest of "the masses" would destroy life as it's lived, life by life. Each person has a story.

This leads to the question of whether generalizing about groups and group behavior is productive. This relates to the military theory debate: the West Point theory and the Sandhurst theory and the playing fields of Eton that produced all the famous British generals versus Tolstoy's idea that what war was really about was one guy on one horse, falling in the mud, looking at the smoke, and having no sense of the general's a priori format, and of how he fitted in—that the cavalry was here and the infantry is there was a theory of masses, not of a single life. **The tension between the two sides of that argument is important to the Gnostic discussion. It's impossible to make circumstances intelligible in the world strictly by talking about groupings, numbers, or tendencies that obliterate the idiosyncrasies, or the nuances of the individuals who are in the group.** Since I don't live my life collectively, that individuated personal aspect has to be acknowledged. The Gnostic argument has to do with the conception of knowledge arrived at in an internal, private, introverted way, not something which is taken off a loudspeaker addressing a crowd of fifteen thousand people where everybody congratulates one another about how wise each of them is, and how everybody else in the world is an idiot.

BROOKS BROTHERS

A slightly disheveled character, Brooks Brothers-ish coat and tie, looking around to decide whether he wants to go with vitamins, or shock, or biofeedback, or meditation. The confusion of life and **the difficulty of finding venues or avenues that make the less intelligible more intelligible. You can find people, some motivated by kindness and convictions and some more mercantile, who will tell you the key to alleviating confusion.** My experience is that there is no single key because there is no single lock. The problem

may be deciding on an allegiance which, in many cases, vilifies other plausible alternatives. There's an **argument for not accepting everything in total but for accepting pieces of things, in different weights, at different times, and for continually reevaluating,** adding and eliminating, not necessarily **with the idea that you would ever arrive at a conclusion which would be final** and which would explain everything, but that the personal paradigm could shift, and one would be willing to accept that. There's a quote by Reinhold Niebuhr, a religious thinker in the middle years of this century who said something which is now on every subway wall. Everybody knows it; whether everybody can put it into effect is a different matter. But Niebuhr's remarks have to do with **the need to have the courage to understand and change what can be understood and changed, and to let go what can't be effected, and to know the difference between the two prospects.** There's a funny line from Kant: "From the crooked timber of humanity no straight thing could ever be made." But crooked, if it were a path for living, would be positive.

BUDDHA

This overgrown Buddha is somewhat like the tree growing out of **Angkor Wat**. Remember, it was the Buddha who admonished us not to build statues, images of him. Someone, apparently wasn't listening. The statue was built, contrary to the recommendation, and time is devouring the result. Siddartha Gautama surely appreciated that force that seems to be continually producing and devouring as the planet metamorphoses. Something keeps pushing up, pushing up the new, turning over, devouring the old. The admonition is simply to be conscious that if you don't mow your lawn it will swallow you—quite literally. That sense of time moving is an aspect of Gnostic architecture. Put another way, architecture should include the Buddha devoured by the forest.

CAGE

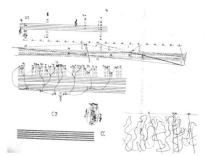

A John Cage score, choreographed visually. Whatever John Cage learned about writing music was apparently inadequate. Therefore he had to amend the form. What he did was to make decisions about what one hears based on what he sees. It's a graphic association of notes connecting points with lines, and points with other points visually, so that the visual esthetic of the music has a substantial role in determining what the music is. And the ear takes the consequences. Cage is asking what music is. Is it what is composed, is it what is played, is it what we hear, is it what is heard and remembered, or is it what one sees? That visual aspect would have to apply, at least, to the musicians who would be able to see his score.

CARACOL

A building almost foreign to the Uxmal context, we might call the Caracol an observatory. But it was as much a religious structure. Its use seems to have been to solve the mysteries of the skies, to map the skies, and to communicate that pattern, that predictable pattern, to the local population. The only building in the Yucatán so far discovered which has a roof dome and a circular plan. The section is quite complicated— helix and dome together. A unique building with a unique purpose which we probably can't account for in terms which made it intelligible to the Mayans. So we try to define it in terms we recognize. The exegesis by the local docents is that the building was designed to track the behavior of Venus in the sky; but the extraordinary power, the physicality of the building and the relative weakness of Venus in the sky don't seem to square. The building is also apparently related to a 52 year cycle, after which the process repeated. There is a theory (however wild) that Venus, according to both Indo-European and Middle-Eastern myths, was born out of the head of Jupiter, rocketing around the sky, possibly as a comet, for a period of time and threatening the earth. I don't know how plausible an idea that is scientifically, although the force of the building seems to warrant a powerful explanation—like a culture facing imminent disaster. A purely cerebral conception of astronomy is ours, not theirs.

CARACOL, DOME

Detail of the dome of the Caracol. The Venutian religious observatory in the Yucatán. An absolutely unique configuration in a society which developed systematic wall and section configurations that were applied to a variety of building types—almost a standardized building system. And then comes this unprecedented anomaly with its astro-religious purpose, housing the observers in the building, who watched the sky so that the society could be informed and protected. A unique building type; a unique purpose; and intentionally antithetical to the surrounding typology. Purposeful contradiction of antecedents has a long civic pedigree.

CEMETERY CITY

From Mumford's *The Myth of the Machine*. There is the city and the cemetery and the question of whether the life of the city is a life that points to death and violence and destruction. The City of Life or the City of Death. Conceivably the Madison Avenue **Race** or **O Happy Days** existence. Everyone running nowhere after nothing. Or the ubiquitous machine as driver and the citizens of the city as simply passengers. The city has to make room for what is private, and personal and imaginative—for the inhabitant to invest a piece of his life. If it's all proscribed and supra-personal it's the City of Death.

CHAPLIN

Chaplin on the wheel. Memories of **Berkeley** in 1967, 1968 with Mario Savio hyperbolizing in Sproul Plaza: how to throw your body on the gears of the odious academic machine. Chaplin reflects on the primacy of the human who once made the machine and is now dwarfed by it, in awe of what he did, which is liable to run away with him. In contemporary architecture the machine and gears have become, in the hands of some, an idol. The machine aesthetic ignores the fragile sensibility it had when it first tentatively arose in the hands of Jean Prouvé early in the century, science and its technical progeny tied to a belief in progress—heat the houses, light the streets, zip around in automobiles. What was difficult is now easy, and everybody is happier as a consequence.

Time and change and progress were conceived explicitly in opposition to an earlier perception of order, constancy, and stability. There was a new clientele: previously the aristocracy, the monarch, the church were the clients; now it is the people. And the analogue machine making the happy city for the people. And then the machine, an end in itself, enamored of its efforts, and Chaplin intervening or contesting the primacy of the depersonalized, institutionalized, bureaucratic machine. I can't talk about "the masses." I can only talk about living—one life at a time. Gnostic architecture has to do with a perception that one by one, one can amend the perception of what's real so one is not run over or devoured by the metaphysical machine. This doesn't deify the antithesis of the machine. It's not a way of saying machines aren't productive or able to make some things better sometimes. It's more conceptually neutral. What the machine is is what we say it is, not what it says we are.

CHICHÉN ITZÁ

The first image is up on a podium where sacrifices were made in the Chacmol, the second is the end of an impossible stair up the face of the pyramid. The two are physically close and both open to the sky. The sky is the roof.

I remember going to see an exhibition in L.A. on the Mayans. The exhibit characterized the Mayans as the Greeks of the New World. The exhibit makers framed the prowess of the Yucatán by associating it with a pedigreed portion of Western History.

The intellectual primacy of the West is shaking. Not because something has overcome it; but because it distrusts itself now. Confidence in its invention—empirical logic—is shaken. Perhaps a more ecumenical view is coming. At the moment though there are just pieces, from a variety of sources. No glue. My experience wandering through the Yucatán is not so different from my travels to Stonehenge. I felt an enormously powerful, elemental quality. Foreign to Western culture. Both a huge confidence and a huge apprehension about how fragile is the order of things. A confidence in how to deal, how to survive. That's a force I love to see in building. It's contagious. That confidence can carry the culture. But not ours. We have too many oppositions and antipathies. In Chichén Itzá one can run a certain homogeneous distance. So different from our time. Not so cerebral and intellectual and studied and analyzed and methodological and calculated and measured and quantified, although it finds ways to make a place for all that secondarily.

THE CONSCIENCE OF WORDS

One shall seek nothingness only to find a way out of it and one shall mark the road for everyone.

-Elias Canetti, from "A Conscience of Words"

This could be a Gnostic paradigm. It's a statement of the moral imperative driving Canetti's intellect and his art. That is, one might wander into nihilism looking for ways to formulate a pattern, a ladder, a road, a rope out—now I'm thinking of the rope quote, "Two feet lower and a halo becomes a noose." In Canetti's terms the poet's task is to take an inherited conceptual model apart, and to leave a record of the disassembled or reassembled pieces so that others who come later to the same ground could find support in his efforts. That wouldn't necessarily mean that the next poet would go further or that there was really a "further" to go, each new attempt at understanding might proceed to the same place but by a different route. The poet's moral imperative is to "make the road" for whoever wants to make that run.

COURAGE

I have the courage, I believe, to doubt everything; I have the courage, I believe, to fight with everything; but I have not the courage to know anything; not the courage to possess, to own anything.

A statement of self-confidence. A statement of humility. To make a building I have to own a paradigm temporarily. By owning I mean conceptualizing an allegiance or hypothesis as space. But while it's constructed it's simultaneously contested, put up, pulled down, like Penelope's quilt—together and apart.

Assembly includes disassembly. But the object is not to return to zero. The object is not to claim permanent residence. This is a transient's paradigm.

CREATION IS A PATIENT SEARCH

The original sketch comes from Le Corbusier. It advocates a balance, half a head of Apollo on the left, half a head of Dionysus on the right; bilaterally symmetrical. The Apollonian aspect is cerebral, rational. The Dionysian aspect represents spirit and psyche—the soul. Measured and unmeasured again.

I rotated the drawing 90 degrees so the figure of Dionysus is the underpinning, and Xerox reduced Apollo, so the rational aspect is a tiny speck floating in the huge Dionysian sea. The intention is to communicate that rationality is an anomaly in something much bigger. **Dionysus and Apollo** no longer equals. Apollo the exception: Dionysus the dominant role.

DEGAS

Ballerinas. The painting suggests the possibility of alternative kinds of balance. There is the balance of standing firmly—a durable balance. Then there is the fragile, delicate balance—one that clearly won't be sustained. For the ballerina, the more tenuous the balance, the more artistic the performance. And we already know the limits of that precarious position. We know the conclusion at the beginning. It doesn't have a long life, but it has a power because of the delicacy and the lack of durability. I think that poignancy, created by **the tension between the time of implementation and the instant of collapse** is very clearly a concern. Gnostic architecture should communicate, in the language of its spaces, the ballerina's dialectic.

DIONYSUS AND APOLLO.

> Here, when the danger to his will is greatest, art approaches as a saving sorceress, expert at healing. She alone knows how to turn these nauseous thoughts about the horror or absurdity of existence into notions with which one can live.
>
> - Friedrich Nietzsche

Commentary from Friedrich Nietzsche, in *The Birth of Tragedy*. The two polemical poles, Dionysus and Apollo, or by a crude extrapolation, Eros and intellect, cerebral and emotional, art and science—perhaps even yin and yang. So when the film viewer is with Kurosawa alone at the top of the mountain in ***Ran***, or with Bruegel staring bewildered at the ***Triumph of Death***, or following **Canetti** in and out of nothingness, or trembling with Michelangelo on the back wall of the **Sistine Chapel**, or misunderstanding with **Kierkegaard** who laughs at his tears and cries at his laughter, art (in the most ecumenical sense) arrives with a very particular mission: to assuage a debilitated, diminished human capacity to go on. As T.S. Eliot wrote in *The Four Quartets* (quoting Krishna): "Not fare well, but fare forward voyagers."

FACE

An almost blank, almost featureless face. Unless you're an expert, it's difficult to tell whether the statue is quite old, or relatively contemporary. I use the statue as a **metaphor for conceptual strategizing in architecture**. If life is a blank face, one has to make the face or assign the face certain features in order to proceed, in order to say what life is. If there's no intrinsic face, then assigning features is not only problematic, but you have to wonder about the longevity of the features that you assign. So the metaphor becomes one of acknowledging the responsibility for the features of the face, and anticipating that the features would

change, so that **the paradigm is not a fixed paradigm** but an evolving or developing or shifting paradigm. Sometimes subtly, sometimes radically. I used to say that life was a blank face, but it's never entirely blank. There are always at least some residual consequences from the previous guy's assignment of features. To assign features, you have to erase the preceding features. **As a more general pattern of behavior, in order to do something I have to move something that preceded me out of the way.**

THE FALL OF ICARUS

The Bruegel painting, *Landscape with the Fall of Icarus*. The dream of flight: Icarus with his melted wax wings falling into the sea, and everyone else paying no attention. He falls, he drowns, everybody goes on, perhaps afraid to look. Special efforts sometimes disappear.

FOUCAULT'S PENDULUM

Randomly they throw in manuscript pages on hermetic thought. The Masters of the World, who live beneath the earth. The Comte de Saint-Germain, who lives forever. The secrets of the solar system contained in the measurements of the Great Pyramid. The Satanic initiation rites of the Knights of the Temple. Assassins, Rosicrucians, Brazilian voodoo. They feed all this into their computer, which is named Abulafia (Abu for short), after the medieval Jewish cabalist.

This is a quote taken from the jacket of *Foucault's Pendulum*, by Umberto Eco, which may indicate someone thought this snippet was compelling advertising. It makes available, in an abbreviated way, qualities I find essential in defining the contemporary philosophical/historical condition, the intellectual conditions which prevail at the moment. There is an enormous amount of empirical information available to us now, more than ever—anthropological, archeological, historical, from diverse places and diverse times: Brazilian Voodoo, the Comte de Saint-Germain, Rosicrucians, Crusaders. Every place, any time. We know about each of these subjects. We know of them as parts without a whole. So the proposed solution here (which is of course not really the solution) is to jam it all into the cabalistic computer which will magically make it all coherent. We have information we've never had, but we don't have any idea how to assemble the pieces, how to value one part relative to another, how to prioritize. History as an impenetrable mosaic of pieces that don't currently fit, but might later on. The theme of possible fit is very much the focus of Eco's novel. For Eco there's an incredibly complicated, delicate, poignant, precarious, almost but not quite decipherable, connecting tissue or sinew or web that might possibly unite all the pieces. Might. We can't detect it today; but tomorrow could be different. The fact of parts and the aspiration to coherence, that the pieces would confirm a continuity as well as the more readily felt discontinuity; **that tension between possibilities is where Gnostic Architecture begins.**

BUCKMINSTER FULLER

Dome over midtown. That has an appeal, if only a perverse appeal. It also has an enormous confidence, an innocent's confidence. This would be the wheel without **Chaplin** on it—the machine that lights the houses, heats the houses and zips the populace around in cars. The world moves forward as a consequence of our ability to apply and deify technology. Again, a huge constructed piece where people are understood in number, not in nuance. As Johnson once said, "Don't try to put a door in a Buckminster Fuller dome." There's no room for personal entry and exit in that technological vision.

GEOLOGY I

A vast piece of geology. What it shows are eons of change, sometimes wild steps in the history of geology, vast cuts and jumps that suggest a more cataclysmic theory of evolution. If I were to argue that architecture has to read and re-direct such geologic revisionism, then this sense of the world moving by jumps, not according to a single, synchronized system, should find its way into architecture. It's plausible to argue that architecture should not deal with painful subjects. That it's job ought to be to add solace and comfort and stability, and put its occupants at ease. That might be part of the job, part of the time; but if that were all of the job all of the time, architecture would divorce itself from subject matter that might lead the culture somewhere else. Architecture would be reactionary, not progressive. A place to hide, as opposed to seek. And architecture is not a place to hide.

GEOLOGY II

A cliff and a spectacular cliff dwelling. Human beings clinging to the layers of geology accumulated over eons. People picking holes in rocks. One could imagine some colossal storm which would wash all human traces away. But the precariousness of the rock habitations, the fragility of it, is its beauty as well as its tension. I was thinking about the "preserve the environment" subject, protecting the environment instead of digging into it. The sense that the earth has to be treasured is coming back again after a long time. The first time around in very primitive civilizations, the earth overwhelmed its peoples. The wind blew you away, the snow froze you, the flood washed you out, and the animals ate you or chased you up trees. It was all too much. The war between man and the environment has been a long one, arriving at the point psychologically where you could plough the snow, put the animals in the zoo, and put the flood in some concrete channel. There are, of course, always cracks in the concrete. But in general, it's possible to make a life absent of those apprehensions of nature. We feel like masters of everything, and now comes the concern that we've pushed too far, and lost that awe of nature. So we look for a way to retrieve it. It's hard to do that without recognizing that the environment itself, however you characterize it, not only washed its inhabitants away for millennia, but breaks itself up and remakes itself in perpetuity. That asteroid collision on **Jupiter** for instance. It's not only human beings that disrupt the environment but the environment, in a cataclysmic way sometimes, disrupts and destroys itself. Why is one of those acceptable, even welcome, and the other one intolerable?

GOD

God isn't dead, survey shows

The local gentry was polled to determine the existence of the deity. Another case where numerology may have nothing to do with the answer, that the answer may be precluded because of the way the question was posed. I think the next question is not whether God is dead, but whether Man is dead. At least in terms of man's ability to come to some kind of terms with a conception of God that a pollster couldn't unravel.

GOD THE GEOMETER

This medieval drawing is another instance, I think, of a culture exteriorizing itself, and calling the result God. The culture's priorities become God's priorities. This could also be identified as a medieval prayer for order. So this is how the world was made, is made, will be made—with a compass, geometry, number and logic, organized in an analytical way. The world is created using Euclid's tools. So, if one knows Euclid, one can provide an exegesis for the design of the cosmos, including the deity. Order can make life plausible, if God behaved as he's represented, and if you subscribe to this depiction. Of course, there is always the apprehension that God won't behave this way at all. When that apprehension is sufficiently strong, along comes the next deity.

HAPPY DAYS

The values of a suburban lifestyle. Gods provided. Culture homogenized. An orderly, well behaved, and predictable road map for living. But happy isn't always happy. And what's happy architecture? Not to invent? Not to investigate? Not to speculate?

THE HELMET

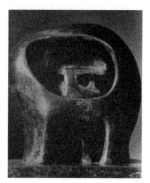

One of the Helmet series of Henry Moore, the exegesis of which explains the structure of this book. A conventional helmet is a protective surround. The exterior form conforms to what it encloses interiorly. The two objects, the inside (head—eyes, ears, nose, mouth) and the outside (helmet) are essentially concentric; the inside of one confirms the outside of the other. Henry Moore's version is somewhat more complicated. There is an external object sufficiently perforated with face-like holes that one can see that it encloses or surrounds or protects something else. But the interior shielded shape isn't coincident with the outer, as is the case with the traditional helmet. It is separated from the exterior and distinct in configuration. The inside shape is wrapped by the external form but the two are separated and different in shape. Here's the exegesis: as with this book, **there's the outside of the outside form, the inside of the outside form and then a space in a perpetual tension. Then there's the outside of the inside form and, finally, the inside of the inside form.** The sculpture could serve as a psychological model for perpetual unraveling, in the sense that one could continue to go further and further in. More pieces, more spaces, more tensions. So the model can be understood as either finite or infinite. The Helmet is also an esthetic amalgam for the relationships between objects. **Outside and inside are both coincidental and discontinuous. Fit and misfit.**

HYBRID MONSTER

This creature stands with many companions along a funeral road near Beijing. On the way to death and on the way from death. Why monsters, one culture after another? Are they psychologically real? Do they reflect the psychological deficiencies of any culture's attempt to represent a world order? Could the monster stand for what we don't know, can't reach, but can at least vaguely imagine? Can architecture include the "can't know" or the "dimly known?"

ISE SHRINE

This is the shrine at Ise near Kyoto. It's a Taoist shrine which goes back to the seventh century AD. It was actually introduced to me by Kenzo Tange who was a professor of mine in 1971. In quite a literal way, the shrine posits two sites, one vacated, and one where the temple is constructed. The built temple stands for

twenty years. After twenty years, it is rebuilt in the identical way, with new materials, on the adjacent site. This continues in perpetuity. So the building is fixed, constant, unmoving, eternal and at the same time is ephemeral, changing, and limited. Ise is both in time and out of time, literally embodied. I once gave a presentation called "the square with no corners." That's a quotation from the Taoist philosopher, Lao Tsu. The Ise shrine is an effort to build physically what the square with no corners implies spiritually. It might be easy to have no corners and it might not be hard to have a square, but the square with no corners is a tough one for **God the Geometer**. And it shows that philosophy can't be translated, syllable by syllable, to building.

JAIPUR

A detail from the public plaza in Jaipur. This Mogul construction belongs to the 18th century. There are series of these sky measuring devices in the plaza, constructively informing the public about the precise relationship between earth and sky. Months, days, years, holidays—time and the movement of the earth, as part of the observable order, part of a perceived mechanism. Astronomy for the citizens as well as the scientists. The tools for this public presentation of astronomy are very tactile, not abstract and cerebral. And the components of the plaza are colossal in scale. When I proposed the Vesey Street project for Battery Park, a publicly accessible cosmology was integral to the project. The Samitaur building, in a different manner, has the hourglass as metaphor for the form of the entry stair. The grains of sand are the people moving up and down the stairway of the entry stair configuration. So it is a time reversing hour glass. Time moves backwards and forwards here. The question of time and cosmology needn't be so solemn. I have an interest in bringing that subject matter to architecture, happy and sad. Man connected with the earth and time, and man disowned by the same parties. Around and around and around.

JOYCE

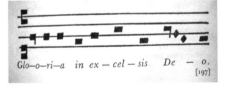

Glo—o—ri—a   in ex — cel — sis   De — o.
[197]

The literary application of a musical score from Joyce's *Ulysses,* the dissolution of boundaries, a visually composed notation for music, and a musical staff and score as literature. The traditional compositional rules are gone—no more capital letter, noun, verb, and period sentence structure. No longer music as simply listening. That language—a form, a way of understanding and communicating is taught and learned or received, inherited and internalized by students does not mean the language is intrinsically *the* language. The form of language may be only extrinsic when it's inherited.

Joyce took Homer's 2,800 year old original story and remodeled it. He moved the document to a different time, not necessarily by erasing it all, but by using Homer as the frame of reference on which Joyce laboriously elaborated.

The music for God, as part of the text, like **Cage,** it's not something that you read and comprehend only intellectually. It's visual. Like e.e. cummings stringing letters and words all over the page. But the line between music and literature has stretched and blurred to encompass new conceptual options. Therefore, the question of what music is or what literature is or what, by implication, architecture is, is open. There is no dictionary. Those who are inclined invent. A door, a wall, a roof, a window, a space is no longer pre-determined.

JUPITER

A photograph from *Time* recently of Jupiter devastated, struck by an enormous asteroid. Whose calendar predicted that event? If I extrapolate from the asteroid strike to the legend of Venus tracked by the priests of the **Caracol** I could arrive at an intrinsically unstable world or unstable world view, as opposed to a predictable, measurable planetary system. Like the story in *The New York Times* that suggests that the **Amazon** River used to flow in the opposite direction and perhaps reversed direction in an instant, not over eons. I don't know if any of this is so, but it has a plausible logic for me. The belief that change could happen in a moment, rather than imperceptibly over millennia, might again be man making himself comfortable, creating a world that he can measure against his own needs—sequential, logical-step-by-step. We can decipher and predict, we can anticipate, as opposed to uh oh, here comes the asteroid. Evolution conceived in discontinuous jumps, not necessarily systematic steps. Asteroids on Jupiter, not Darwin on Earth.

KIERKEGAARD

Kierkegaard was the author who admonished his readers not to quote him at all—not to break the seamless fabric of his text—so this quotation is sacrilege. Does it follow that no real understanding is ever possible? Or does it follow that if one dismantles his current misunderstanding that a true understanding can be arrived at? Suppose we really have everything backwards or upside down? An understanding, a stance seems to be necessary to proceeding in the world, and yet our ordering ideas seem consistently inadequate. What if up were really down, or right were really wrong. Kierkegaard also said "so also what I write contains the notice that everything is to be understood in such a way that it is revoked, that the book has not only an end but a revocation." So understanding is and isn't. I sometimes feel that the self-confidence, the energy, the intellectual prospect of saying this is the way it is, knowing no source outside myself, is sufficient. I don't think this is arrogance although it might be misread as if it were, because simultaneously I feel I can't do it, can't reach it, and I'll never get it. This isn't cynicism or negativity or nihilism, none of those.

What if everything in the world were a misunderstanding, what if laughter were really tears?

- Kirkegaard

In architectural terms what I've proposed is an intentional oxymoron, the dialectical lyric. The dialectic suggests the intellectual tension in Kierkegaard's quote, but the lyric would allow a different experience beyond this contradiction. That doesn't eliminate the dialectic in an intellectual way but it might allow one to transcend it in a spiritual way. **This is architecture as religion in the most ecumenical sense, which is Gnostic architecture's first sense.**

KLEE

This painting by Paul Klee is actually a city planning subject, perhaps unintended by the artist. It can be understood as a representation of how the city reflects itself, extends itself, re-engenders itself. How does the modern city enlarge, extend, replace its pieces, re-invent what it is, or what it might mean? The city can't extend itself by mirroring its history narcissistically. The city can't fall too deeply in love with its reflected image or it drowns in regressive planning. We have to find **a way of acknowledging the essential residual consequences of yesterday in order to push or to move the definition of the city beyond its memory.** This is recollecting forward, which is precluded by simply memorializing yesterday.

LENIN

Тов. Ленин ОЧИЩАЕТ
землю от нечисти.

This Constructivist poster is not unrelated to the **Prince of Wales:** Lenin sweeping out the villains—bankers, monarchs, priests—*The Three Penny Opera's* diabolical characters. The association between political allegiances and esthetic vantage points is rare in the United States, but strong in Europe. I'm not for the allegiances, but I am for the sense that architecture is deeper than esthetic strategies. Politics isn't deep enough either, or personal enough; you have to be private before being public. A cast of angelic characters and villains won't do it. Which is not to say that the politics of the architect are the politics of his work. They might be quite different from one another, regardless of what the architect claims.

LURKING MONSTER

Counting the boards on the fence. Like counting cracks in a sidewalk. Who's the lurking monster? Who's the apprehensive counter? Do monsters only appear in the cracks or should monsters be counted along with the planks? Is the monster part of the order or out of order? Maybe what's required is a way of conceptualizing architecture that includes its demons. Meaning, a way of representing space that incorporates antipathies. Or perhaps the monster was simply imagined.

MACHU PICCHU

Perhaps related to the early images of Samitaur and those regularly irregular, almost orthogonal blocks that have to be tamed and strapped together. The early piecemeal building was strapped together. Otherwise the whole assembly would burst. Like **Patfard Clay's** student union, it seems audacious, but in a different way than San Francisco State. It's enormous walls and huge stones represent inexorable power and a colossal effort to move. It had to be there; it had to be done. But this is a societal effort, a cultural decision, by what slaves or free people, by what priestly or monarchical admonitions I don't know. But the audacity is collective as opposed to the San Francisco State student union which is more private, more precarious, in a time when there is no collective audacity. There is a collective skittishness and conservatism—better weigh it, better measure it, better analyze it and, in the end, like J. Alfred Prufrock, it's a life measured out with coffee spoons.

THE MADMAN

Years ago I used this painting by Courbet as an introduction to a lecture. I remember saying, "This architecture is the act of a desperate man." That sounds a little melodramatic. I don't think I was quite prepared to say that the architecture was the act of a madman. This discussion reminds me of a remark by Chesterton,

a British ironist, who claimed that, "the madman is the man who has lost everything but his reason." **I used this subject matter to suggest that architecture is generated from a precarious psychological state, existing in a dialectical tension,** without any paradigmatic allegiance. The need was to sustain a number of contradictory (maddening?) possibilities simultaneously. I could never become the man who arrives at an intersection where there are multiple roads leading in and out and insists there is only one way to move. The option to go down several roads at once and, if required, come back to the origin, must be sustained. Continuing along a single road so that ultimately, the other roads are forgotten is not an option that interests me. The architect documents his own journey. The prospect of going down all roads is inconceivable—who could know them all? But I want to remain conscious that other possibilities are as real.

MOON MAP

A map of the moon from Caltech or MIT. An indication of a certain way of understanding. Our way. Our time. It's a map of a piece of the moon with a grid imposed. Based on the assumption that the Cartesianizing of the surface is synonymous with the development of an understanding of that surface. To grid something, to geometrize a surface is to begin to comprehend according to this premise. The grid does give a measurable legibility; but is legibility, numbers and dimensions, commensurate with understanding? The moon doesn't give a damn about our grid. The grid has more to say about the people who are imposing it, who claim it's a way of objectifying what's external to them. But it's only a way of subjectively interpreting how we define what is objective. I could say measuring objectifies. But I think the idea of measuring leaves out the important immeasurables. I did a lecture which, stealing from Kafka's Diary, I called *Coughing Up the Moon*. That was Kafka's metaphor for the creative process. The moon grid is anathema to the coughing up the moon metaphor. Kafka's image is out of reach of the grid. In fact, the more moon you grid, the less moon you cough up. I don't know whether the two sensibilities could run together. To be conscious of both is to know the insufficiency of either. But for the moment this is simply a point about the limits of the grid-mind and the subjectivity of what is claimed to be objective, subjectivity not being a pejorative term.

MUSTANG II BOREDOM 0

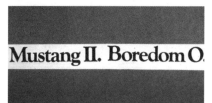

An old advertisement that is probably self-explanatory. The proposition is that the problems of a short attention span can be resolved by the continuing purchase of novelties. Life experience as commodity. You have to buy the next one and the next one and there's never an end. The ultimate solution is never a prospect because that would mean you could stop buying. Culture with an outside but no inside. Culture determined externally which suggests an empty inside. Not uncoincidentally, our most powerful built symbols, high-rise buildings, are like that. The image, the power, is an extroverted manifestation of potency, not the 9 foot floor heights into which the occupants are stuffed. Madison Avenue sells buildings with outsides and no insides.

NAZGA

The plains of Nazga. A very large desert, in the Peruvian highlands. Massive cuts in the stone surface of the desert, colossal etchings in the ground which can't be read clearly from the ground, only from the sky. Presumably addressed to a natural force or to a deity who could understand or read from on high. I would liken this to **God the Geometer**. A culture which starts primitively, and doesn't know how to order itself, how to organize its life, what to value, what to genuflect toward, and therefore, starts to imagine the world

ordered and organized according to a particular strategy. God the Geometer tells us that God works with precision, with tools, so life can be analyzed, has a method, has a sequence. It's the way a culture teaches itself what the primary qualities of living are, or what issues are to be addressed, and in what form. The institutions and their physical symbols are established, etched in the cultural psyche. Insisted on. It's an aspiration for permanence. The culture first invents itself, then looks to itself for what to do. Like the **Face** with no features. This is a prayer for order. One invents Nazga, then goes to Nazga and asks what to do. Something psychologically intriguing about that step. A little disingenuous? First you invent out of your experience, you give forms, give order, provide symbols and rules. Then you ask the rules you made how to value, how to behave. In the end you're always asking yourself. Once you feel that, you get suspicious of following anybody else's rules.

OLD STONES

I remember a conductor on the train to Salisbury Plain referring to the "old stones." He said, "Are you going to see the Old Stones?" You can't get there now. There's a fence around the Old Stones. Maybe not so old. There's a power and confidence. It's more instinct, culture as instinct first, which doesn't mean it has no intellectual component, but intellect as the handmaiden of instinct. Contemporary cosmology comes out of the barrel of near-sighted telescopes. Stonehenge represents both great fear and great confidence. All this effort to circumscribe the gods, to get them to listen and to hear. Whether it's Stonehenge or pyramids in the Yucatán, Tiahuanaco, and Egypt, the whole society seems to roll its energies, its survival, into the construction. But the primacy of that attempt at a stable relationship—man to God in the cosmos—is reflected in the magnitude of the stones. Floated down the river, and dragged huge distances. The ultimate effort. What stands from different periods is a good measure of how that culture valued what it built. What is made from stone and what from sticks tells the story. Where are our old stones?

PARIS

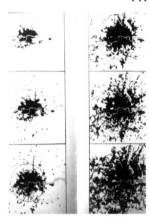

This comes from a city planning book from the 60s or 70s, *Constantine Doxiadis*. It's tiny Paris in the Seine, growing rapidly onto both banks over a relatively short period of time. Do architects have the ability to evaluate the growth of cities and the organization of cities and anticipate urban organizational questions that would redirect the growth of cities in some intelligible form, or do they inevitably run behind forces they can only provide a tentative exegesis for in retrospect? The city theory is always behind what actually is happening to the city, which continues to outrun us at a faster and faster pace. Particularly cities like Mexico City and Seoul and Manila and Taipei. Cities that are not recognizable as identifiable parts of a coherent whole and have no apparent stopping points. Just constant movement. A flood of elements shoved together and apart, growing and expanding; removing and replacing; amending and remodeling at an astonishing and exciting rate—a rate which is not controllable in a measured, systematic, methodological, sequential way. It's a growth which always outruns our ability to account for it.

PATFARD CLAY

A building that was done by the architect who I really consider my only real teacher. The architect was a man named Patfard Keatinge Clay, I met him when I was a student and he was a teacher at Cal Berkeley. He worked in Le Corbusier's office in the late 40s on Marseilles and on Ronchamp. Then he came to the United States and he was at Taliesen with Wright for a short period. Then he worked at Skidmore Owings

and Merrill in Chicago for awhile. And then he started his own practice in San Francisco which ran for maybe 10 years. Later on he went to Spain. We've corresponded sporadically since.

The building is the student union at San Francisco State, a three-story frame with triangular base—lots of open space within the frame and various odd pieces that can be put in or taken away. Conceptually there's the fundamental order, and then the more ephemeral programmatic parts are added or subtracted. At the top of this three-story poured concrete frame is a big deck. The students can go up on the deck and run around. Then out of the deck come two flying tetrahedrons, pointing to the sky. One contains a student lounge, and the other has group meeting spaces and a small theatre. The tetrahedrons emerge from the primary structure. What I admired about the building was its audaciousness. It's a striking form, unfettered by anything around it. Its conviction that it was worthwhile to make this very particular kind of space is remarkable. Parenthetically, and a little bit sadly, I think the deck or the tetrahedrons, or at least one of the tetrahedrons has been closed down because it wasn't designed to be accessible to the handicapped. I think this was done in a period when there was a transition between the development of building rules for the handicapped and no such rules at all. How that circumstance has been adjudicated I don't know, but the project remains an extremely potent space for architecture, and a clear non-sequitur. It was carried forward strictly by the conviction of the architect, there's no precedent for that sort of effort in San Francisco or on the campus of San Francisco State.

THE PETAL HOUSE

This is a photograph that Tim Street-Porter shot from the Santa Monica freeway 15 years ago. I always liked this photo—the house in the foreground against the background of those two towers in Century City. The photo is a dramatic representation of relative vantage points. From here the Petal House appears large and the towers small. How do projects of an imposing scale impact the city? Meaning, the relation of size to impact—what's the relationship? And how do we value the meaning of that small building against the kind of power and authority which is often represented in the contemporary city by these enormous buildings. The plan form of the two towers is triangular and the pieces of the opened roof, the roof of the Petal House, are also triangular, so there was, in one sense, something strangely similar about the two projects.

PHOBOS

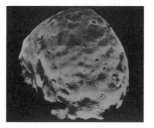

A Martian moon called Phobos. Interests me for a couple of reasons. One is that the image is beautiful, a precise and imprecise piece of rock, approaching a sphere but also moving away. The moon rotates retrograde, so it rotates in the wrong direction according to all the theories that were voguish when this discovery was made. According to the Big Bang concept all the planets and the moons appeared at once, with similar ways of moving. **That theory, like many scientific theories which are often represented as durable as a consequence of the fact that they can be quantified, is likely to be replaced rather quickly by another hypothesis.** The social theories we could derive from crowds in **Berkeley** and the behavior of crowds, their allegiances, their vilification of opposition, I feel might be more durable as laws, more dependable than the empirically derived scientific laws. The scientific dictums are precise for very short periods. So they're not precise. This is the real nature of Science's laws, distributed by what I would consider to be the only extant facsimile of a priesthood we have now. **Phobos is not explainable as the scientist's anticipated.** And it's quite striking and beautiful as an object.

PRINCE OF WALES

A headline. Has to do with the Prince of Wales, and what is taught and learned as architecture. And what's taught is often internalized, and then spit out as if what's taught were intrinsically and externally so. Here's the power that certain people have to bring their ideas to bear in the world. That the Prince of Wales is a sponsor, and has the wherewithal to provide a podium, a platform and fiscal credence to make a school, where he could teach that the future is the past. I always thought his message was simply from a character who didn't read enough Charles Dickens before advocating the memorializing of some of the most rancid tendencies in city building in the name of a disingenuous pseudo-progressive conservatism. And it's a hollow resurrection; claiming the past is the future won't work. I think The Prince had an apprehension of a crude contemporarism which is a different flavor of brutality, though it would be possible to attack that superficial modernism without Charles Dickens as an alternate.

PROGRESS

> Faith in progress does not mean progress has occurred. That would be no faith.
>
> Kafka

Kafka doesn't rule out the possibility of an event happening that hasn't happened before and can't be referenced based on precedent. The expression "faith in progress" is only representational of the "true" faith if it represents a confidence that hasn't been sustained by a priori evidence. He doesn't think there is much evidence, but he doesn't want to say no progress, although probably his artistic instinct is "more of the same." It's similar to the image of Kafka's man in *The Trial* facing the Door of the Law over many years, finally dying, and seeing a light shining underneath the door. Maybe a suggestion that what hasn't happened is still possible, at least theoretically. A conclusion, a comprehension of what seems inscrutable, is a perpetual prospect. Gnostic architecture is that prospect. We have all sorts of experiences that seem to suggest that life exists as an infinite number of fragments, and yet there may be a way to jump over those arguments in a language that is not our normal language, to understand that it is possible to come to a different conclusion, **to resolve rather than just dissect.**

PYTHAGORAS

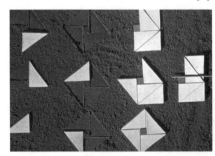

Lines in the sand, illustrating the proportional properties of the Pythagorean theorem: the sum of the squares of the sides of the right-angled triangle being equal to the square of the hypotenuse. The search for fundamental patterns. The essence as mathematical and geometric. Pythagoras and Euclid. We're dealing with a subject which has long been fundamental to architecture, to the ordering of buildings, and the organization of cities. Shapes we can write equations for, elements we can measure—right angles and squares. The quantifiable order of things, the measurable order of things, the perception that a dimensional essence lies at the heart of things.

Life qualified by quantifying. We don't often acknowledge what Pythagoras' diagram has left out. In lectures I sometimes use Rembrandt's painting of *The Sacrifice of Isaac* juxtaposed with Pythagoras in an effort to represent another law and another voice, one that couldn't be understood in terms of Pythagorean logic: no number, measure, analysis, or reading through an electron microscope—a kind of enigmatic "voice of God in the whirlwind" law. And the example was God's insistence that Abraham take his son to Mount Moriah and execute him. In the realm where Pythagoras makes sense, what Abraham was told by God might make no sense. I remember **Kierkegaard** discussing the Abraham/Isaac story, and asking rhetorically, "How many of you does this story keep up at night?" Of course, by implication, it kept Kierkegaard wide awake. Man exteriorizing man in the face of that voice out of the whirlwind. Our culture has tried to insist there's only Pythagoras. But the message to Abraham keeps appearing through the cracks.

RACE

Innumerable **Brooks Brothers** characters running madly after who knows what. This is what used to be referred to euphemistically as the rat race. Hurrying mindlessly after Madison Avenue-determined goals. The extrovert's race as opposed to the introvert's race. The cartoon on the magazine cover, **"O Happy Days"** also deals with the homogeneity of suburban life—what values it teaches and what it also leaves out.

A while ago, Malcolm Muggeridge, an Anglo-Catholic, was discussing totalitarianism with William F. Buckley. They were talking about political and social instincts for totalitarianism, the tyranny of a certain way of thinking, or living, or understanding. Muggeridge referred to the totalitarian tendency metaphorically speaking, to cover the earth with concrete, but inevitably, the concrete cracks, and out of the cracks will come, Alexander Solzhenitsyn. Solzhenitsyn, at that time, was a symbol of resistance, and the impossibility of total tyranny.

RAN I

A watercolor study by Akira Kurosawa for his movie *Ran,* which has, I think, been mistranslated as chaos. Chaos is too simple for Kurosawa. Chaos is too easy for everybody. Instead, there are always threads that interconnect and suggest vaguely the prospect of various kinds of ordering methods. This painting represents a scene at the end of the movie. The man is blind, standing at the edge of a cliff, about to fall, with the world behind him on fire. Everything on fire—spectacular but horrible. In existential terms, sad and disjointed. Not much individual hope. But the prospect that it might work, that the plan might succeed, is always there. And, he made the movie. Perhaps the act of creating the film is itself a positive rejoinder to the film's message that the world is burning.

RAN II

Another image for *Ran.* This isolated character on the edge of the cliff, a silhouette, blind and moving with a cane to disaster at the edge of the cliff. Down below everything is being destroyed by fire. I don't want to leave the subject at the bottom of the cliff, though it's sometimes hard to get beyond that. **Canetti's** comment, "...that one shall seek nothingness in order to find a way out of it," applies here. Kurosawa's process of delivering this image is an effort both to understand the emptiness and, I think to climb over it, perhaps through the art of the film itself. To try, not simply to sink in a psychologically defoliated, physically demolished landscape.

ROCKBUILDING

How to define the act of building? How to prescribe and proscribe the prospect? How to state the limits of architecture? What's a wall, a roof, a door, a floor? This is the rock building. This is the building rock. Nature made and now manicured? Or man-made and nature manicured? The object obviates any conventional definition of man-made.

Eric Owen Moss **43**

ROTHKO

This is a painting from a series by Mark Rothko which has been critical to my interest in expressing the tension between alternative design possibilities, occurring simultaneously, and the awareness that that dialectic might be transcended. But first, as an avant gardist, attempting to modify the language of paint when the antecedent form loses its vitality. This change in form language can take place within a recognized grouping of signs and symbols, colors and techniques; or the new framework might appear outside the current ordering system. There's a mood in Rothko, a need which manifests itself in a constant effort to paint what is uniquely personal. At the same time, what intrigues me is the possibility that what he invented also had a generic applicability. The discovery is both personal and generic. Therefore, what Rothko conceived becomes another way, another plan, another pattern, another framework, and a contrary proposition to Tolstoy's idea that history only exists one life at a time. Rothko's art is private. Rothko's art is collective.

What I'm interested in postulating is a framework that bridges contrary ideas, a dialectical tension, which might endure precisely because it's allegiance is to a conceptual non-allegiance. The target is to express the stress between allegiances. The Rothko painting, as an example, suggests two prospects. One is that of an orthogonal, or almost orthogonal, vantage point. That position starts with a Euclidean discussion, a previously learned and therefore remembered geometry—one could write an equation for the rectangle, the right angle. But at the same time he suggests a second prospect—the dissolution of the right angle. He shows both possibilities because the edges of the rectangle start to dissolve, and suggest movement in another spatial direction, away from the rectangle we know toward a configuration less definable or yet to be defined. The painting is itself that tension between what we can recall of the orthogonal representation, and away from that same representation. And therefore it embodies the stress by suggesting or proposing or embodying neither position entirely but both partially and simultaneously. **The painting is the dialectical tension in this exegesis.** If the painting is sufficiently powerful and the experience picks you up and moves you along then you live a vital transcendence.

SATURN DEVOURING ONE OF HIS SONS

Goya originally painted this on the wall of his house. Now its in the Prado. It is maybe the most horrifying object I've ever seen. To intellectualize it is to separate oneself from the horror. Saturn is time, not its symbol. Time devours us—ripping the head, swallowing the body. The subject matter is comparable to that character of Michelangelo's, staring at the skull. It's the experience Nietzsche referred to when he talked about what breaks the will. The painting is the salvation of the artist's will. Otherwise Goya goes off the roof.

SCALE

What's the metaphorical meaning of the bent scale? Is objectivity numbered? Is empiricism simply dimension and quantity? What measures can measure? Not measure? What understanding does the scale contribute? What meanings does the scale omit? Can the bent scale measure what the straight scale cannot?

THE SCHOOL OF ATHENS

A piece of a painting by Raphael in the Vatican Museum—what we could label man exteriorizing man. I use it, I'm a part of it. But I can also feel the arrogance. Man looking to assign his methods to God. So that what we've invented doesn't simply belong to us, but is our extension, or investigation, or discovery of an intrinsic order. Now everything works. Euclid's precise fit. A great statement of self-confidence—man can decipher the order. Or a prayer for the efficacy of the methods man invents.

SEVEN SERMONS TO THE DEAD

A Gnostic symbol from early in the Christian era. I found the drawing in a book called *Seven Sermons to the Dead* by Carl Jung. The head of a rooster means light, and the tail of snake references the dark. Light designates understanding and clarity and presumably, dark references the opposite. This diagram signifies both oppositions and the reconciliation of oppositions. Nietzsche's **Dionysus and Apollo** defined oppositions but not the reconciliation. Yin and yang could convey a similar meaning in a more abstract graphic language. The Gnostic life is personal, and not transferable. This isn't an ideology that can be applied collectively. Understanding occurs one person at a time. One by one. Perhaps, it's possible to bridge the light and dark conflict, to resolve the dichotomy. **So the Gnostic experience, in spatial terms, transcends the intellectual dialectic but doesn't eradicate it. The contention of intellectual possibilities remains, but the dialectical poem, the dialectical lyric —Abraxas—makes a different prospect available.**

SISTINE CHAPEL

A portion of the back wall of the Sistine Chapel. Michelangelo looking at what's about to become of him and everyone else. In the Western sense, it's the fundamental existential problem of the limits of everything or the instability of everything, very much the focus of the intellectual history of the twentieth century. Whether it's **Cage**, or Schönberg, or **Joyce**, or Genet. I don't know whether architecture has ever explicitly made that subject its subject, how fragile the experience of living is, one life at a time. **How to build that life tension into architecture is part of the Gnostic aspiration.**

The painting is from the sixteenth century and has contemporary relevance, so even the **Prince of Wales** can be correct. Strangely, almost anyone can be a little bit right. Which leads me away from any permanent allegiance, because as soon as I sign up on one side I've made an opposition of the other side, and in almost every case there's at least something useful on the other side which creates a tension between the two.

This is not an argument for not making a choice, but it is an argument for skepticism about any position held too tightly for too long. Maybe that's where the fear is. Maybe Michelangelo's image might account for the Prince of Wales' stance who, looking over his shoulder, is desperate for a durability which could stand in opposition to the fragile human condition. Now the Eastern vantage point is different. Underneath what seems to change and move is something which is no thing. How to call that, how to touch that without contaminating it? Both experiences are real, both the change and movement (which feels more poignant to me) and the stillness. Maybe I can't get over where I came from, the time and the place. But I'm conscious that there is another possibility that could exist beyond the terror and panic and horror on this face. My retort to Michelangelo could be, "What is all the fuss about?"

SKELETON

All the pieces intact. Reassembled so the surface configuration is implied by the sub-structure. Or is it? **A question of the relationship of support to surface to meaning. Outside to inside. How are they associated? Outside observed on the inside, inside observed on the outside?** Rules for the expression of support to surface? Hierarchy of support parts? A **Helmet** of sorts.

TATLIN

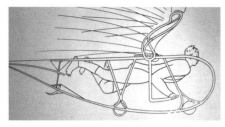

Russian Constructivism and Tatlin's glider. The magic and majesty of flight. Daedalus and Icarus becoming, in the 1920s, technically plausible. How fascinating that what is so compelling about technological advances is only briefly compelling. The wonder at the achievement is as important as the technology. Should a 1500 foot high tower or an airplane traveling 700 miles an hour or the bridge spanning 1500 feet not be an enduring astonishment? And all of that done by the insignificant man whose efforts the trees and grass keep devouring. Perhaps the time span of a single life is inadequate to measure the durability of a particular technical achievement. Perhaps that magnitude is only measurable after the utilitarian purposes are lost or obscured.

From a second vantage point it's curious that a conceptual trail runs from the form language of Constructivism to the form language of Deconstruction. Russian Constructivism, with an ethos of technical optimism and historic progress points, quizzically, to Deconstruction with its perpetual fragments and loss of hope.

TIANAMEN SQUARE

The Tianamen Square event fascinated me. As a student in **Berkeley** in the late 60s, observing crowds and power, and watching those developments in China 25 years later, listening to the rhetoric and watching the unabashed brutality of totalitarian power, and hearing that brute power represented as honorable and the opposition as diabolical. I can remember a 10,000 crowd day in Sproul Plaza on the Berkeley campus, with numberless people speaking vociferously, some eloquently, over a public microphone, criticizing the administration of the University (with justification), and congratulating themselves on their ability to intervene in the University's history in the interest of justice, democracy and freedom. Then one guy got up, I remember he had red hair and a black patch over his left eye. This is 1965. And when he started to speak he was booed. There wasn't much patience with his sympathies which were outside predictably narrow campus allegiances. Heroes and villains seemed predetermined. Not much dexterity of opinion. I could see immediately that certain ambiguities, certain tensions would be lost in the face of the apparent need to polarize positions and insist on the purity of the student vantage point. So this guy jumped up, and started talking from the perspective of persecuted students in Romania. He was a graduate student. He spoke about big black cars coming around corners in Bucharest, and secret police grabbing people off the streets, dragging them into the cars, never to be seen again. Suddenly Bob Dylan's *Sad Eyed Lady of the Lowlands* blared over the loudspeakers. I can't recall any objections to the censoring of a student who had fought tyranny in another place. Testing the belief system is always tough. If an entrenched, established position has to be moved they always resist. I wonder sometimes in discussions with clients and city administrators if the argument and intelligence of particular positions is only a veneer for the relative power positions of the people involved in the debate. That what appears to be a debate about alternate solutions is likely to be decided on the basis of relative power positions. That that is well understood and needn't be stated explicitly. What I love about this anonymous man in front of the tank is the possibility of standing against that force and forcing a retreat—a revision. The man stood for a moment in the face of the tank, and the tank went around. Architecture can sometimes obligate the tank to go around.

TIAHUANACO

A gargantuan archeological piece of undefined origin in Bolivia. The contemporary nomenclature refers to this object as the *Tower of the Sun*. It adjoins Lake Titicaca where a once mighty civilization apparently lies under water. This is a poignant example of forces in history that our conceptions don't yet, and may never, have the capacity to account for. It's very very old, in historical terms. A colossal cut stone construction. The building is pre-Mayan, pre-Inca, pre-everybody as far as we know, which isn't sufficiently far to catalogue the builders in our historical chronology. The scale is astonishing. There it is, enigmatically what we don't know, don't understand, and can't touch. For all our culture's eloquence of knowing and our rhetoric of understanding, when we stand in the face of Tiahuanaco we feel not only its majesty but the inadequacies of our ways of representing it. Who did it? Where did they come from? How have they disappeared? Only marginally accounted for.

TRIUMPH OF DEATH

A Bruegel painting. Here the subject of death is not a general matter but specific to each individual. The painting is enormously complicated. It reminds me of Tolstoy's conception of the writing of history: there is no history, no single direction, only histories. Only individual renditions. What's real is what runs through the life of an infinite number of people, person by person. So to tell the painting's story is to tell it story by story, but in what order? From the top, the side, all at once? The discussion in *War and Peace* of the battle of Borodino is quite different than the same subject studied as a conventional chapter in military history at West Point. The military academy historians would conclude that for tactical reasons the cavalry went here and the infantry went there and the terrain was like this and the battle proceeded in such and such a sequence. A representation of reciprocal strategizing. But Tolstoy represents it from the vantage point of the individual cavalry man, in a ditch, fallen from his horse in the midst of smoke, fire, and mud. There is no supra-personal strategy, only the confused lives of the participants, one by one, only discontinuity. And it's disingenuous, says Tolstoy, to overlay an order, an intellectualization, a nomenclature, a format. This is famously portrayed in Kurosawa's *Roshomon*. I know that some conceptual overlook contributes to the understanding of Borodino and the *Triumph of Death*. But it would be a mistake to neglect

Tolstoy's perception that the history of an event can only be told person by person. Neglecting that view tends to rule out the single conclusions, often requisite to a larger vision.

TURNER

In this is a painting by Turner, done early in the 19th century, the fog is descending, or ascending; one can't determine. The quality of enigma or mystery arrives in Turner's astonishing ability to abrogate the definition of what one sees through the use of color. But this is no single color we could name. Turner's colors are light striking water after a storm. Complex beyond words. The colors suggest a number of perceptual possibilities. The subjects at sea are partly legible, partly illegible; and that ambiguity makes room for the imagination to consider what the fog might be covering, what it might disclose if it lifted. Of course there are **lurking monsters** in the water. There's a Paul **Klee** painting, not dissimilar, with the man in that peculiar boat spearing two sea monsters. Does the clear view always reveal monsters?

UXMAL

I took this photograph standing on the mislabelled Pyramid of the Magician looking out into that infinite green. The jungle is ravenous in the Yucatán. There's a piece of a pyramid and I suspect other buildings, even cities that could be scraped clean there. Architecture keeps moving, not always in the direction you would like. But it's irrepressible. We keep building. But what's also irrepressible is what keeps devouring the buildings. Doctor Doolittle's Push Me Pull You, incognito.

This is a draft of one of five sections from the book **Gnostic Architecture,** by eric owen moss, edited and designed by Group C Inc./New Haven, Boston, USA. This book will be published shortly by Monacelli Press.

Botond Bognar

The Japanese Example – The Other *End* of Architecture

Tadao Ando • Hiroshi Hara • Itsuko Hasegawa •Toyo Ito • Fumihiko Maki •Kazunari Sakamoto •
Kazuyo Sejima • Ryoji Suzuki • Masaharu Takasaki • Kenzo Tange • Riken Yamamoto

"...in dismantling [the buildings] we reversed the process of the construction of architecture. Needless to say, this [was] not a simple act like playing a film backwards. 'Destruction' and 'creation;' can we not say that the effect of an overlapping of incongruous time is the erasure of 'architecture' itself?"
Ryoji Suzuki, *Absolute Scene Tokyo*, 1987[1]

"The places of present-day architecture cannot repeat the permanences produced by the force of the Vitruvian *firmitas*. The effects of duration, stability, and defiance of time's passing are now irrelevant. The idea of place as the cultivation and maintenance of the essential and the profound, of a genius loci, is no longer credible in an age of agnosticism; it becomes reactionary. Yet the loss of these illusions need not necessarily result in a nihilistic architecture of negation. From a thousand different sites the production of place continues to be possible. Not as a revelation of something existing in permanence, but as the production of an event."
Ignasi de Solá-Morales. *Differences* [2]

The issue I intend to discuss here is not architecture's running out of innovative ideas or its recent radical transformation into "obliteration" or its end "as we have known it," but the *time*, when its time is up, when architecture as a *material entity,* for one reason or another, is no longer used and comes to its demise. While the two "ends" are inevitably related and so there are certainly many aspects in which today both ends meet, there is no reason why the "end of architecture" issue could not be approached from the *other end,* that is, where the question is: *how long can or should it last?*

This question is brought into sharper focus by many contradictory forces today; the now necessary, but too often only fashionable, recent movement to create "sustainable" environments is one of them. The other force is, of course, the rapid

progress in technology, which seems to obliterate much of the "built" environment at a delirious pace. Not independent of this, however, is the economy of these states of affairs; the issue therefore is, as almost always, a societal one (life styles or culture, state of the economy, available materials and technologies, and last but not least the political or power relations in a given place and period of time) which guides, if not always determines, the time-frame within which it makes sense to maintain or sustain a piece of architecture, the city, and even the larger environment, in the way they serve the interest of a particular society. And in this respect it is instructive to take a closer look at Japan as a unique example.

[In Japan] buildings are designed in the expectation not that they will stand the test of time but that they will be torn down sooner rather than later and replaced by something more appropriate to the economic and technological demands of the future.
John Thackara, "In Tokyo they shimmer, chatter and vanish"[3]

In 1986 Toyo Ito completed his well-known Nomad Restaurant and Bar in the glitzy Roppongi area of Tokyo; designed in a few weeks; built in less than a few months, it operated for three years before being demolished in 1989. Kazuo Shinohara's famous and much published House in Yokohama, built in 1984, was sold and replaced with another residence in 1994. Masaharu Takasaki's Crystal Light, a company guest house completed in Tokyo in 1986, was hardly used at all before being torn down in 1990. A more prominent case is Kenzo Tange's Tokyo City Hall of 1957 in the city's Marunouchi district; once the new City Hall, also by Tange, was built in Shinjuku in 1991, the old one was torn down in 1992, after only thirty-five years of service. The Tokyo International Forum, designed by Rafael Vinoly, was built on the site of the old hall in 1996. One is also prompted to mention Frank Lloyd Wright's Imperial Hotel in Tokyo, which met its demise not in the 1923 devastating Kanto

Earthquake, which it survived unscathed, but in the frenzy of rapid urban development in the 1960s, when its two-storey structure was replaced by a high-rise hotel.[4]

In a recent conversation, Ito mentioned casually that his well-known U House in Nakano, Tokyo, built in 1976, had just been demolished. Similarly, Minoru Takeyama reported that five of his residential buildings, completed as recently as the 1970s, are no longer standing, having been razed in the past few years.[5] The list can go on and on, including small and large structures, obscure and prominent, even landmark buildings in Japan. And, of course, while many of the demolished structures were dilapidated or outdated, many, as the above examples show, were in good condition.

In Japan, complex conditions and powerful forces challenge any simple understanding about the "normal" course of aging, and necessitate a substantial reinterpretation of the issue of "durability" in architecture and the built environment. Some of these forces are common to many countries, some, particular to Japan.

Japan ... is probably still the world's most technologically advanced and productive nation, of formidable economic power, with an astounding capacity for work, organization, investment, and research, combined with a sense of accuracy and precision in manufacturing which is the result of a very old tradition in which *the values of craftsmanship prevail over the rarity or antiquity of an object.*
Vittorio Gregotti, "Japan: A Disoriented Modernity."[6]

In Japan land is scarce and notoriously expensive, while in Tokyo land prices are skyrocketing.[7] Although they have declined somewhat from the stratosphere of the 1980s (an average of 30%), one square foot of land in the Ginza 5-chome area was worth about $24,000 as recently as 1991.[8] Annual real estate taxes (*koteishizan-sei*), and inheritance taxes or "death-duties" (*sozoku-sei*), are also high, the latter often 60% of the estimated property value. Thus

many would-be owners, such as family heirs, are forced either to sell an entire estate or, after demolishing any building on the site, to sell part of the land to pay the taxes and then to build another profit-generating edifice as fast as possible; to leave land empty is too costly. Such conditions and practices contribute not only to the incessant removal and rebuilding of structures, but also to the progressive fragmentation of the landscape and the city.

The city changes at a dizzying pace defying every attempt at control and planning. This internal, seemingly wilful force of change defines Tokyo.
Judith Connor Greer, "Tokyo in Transition."[9]

The average building in large and expensive urban areas costs only about 10% of the land on which it stands. Relative to the value of the land, then, construction is cheaper in Japan than anywhere else; this results in more renovation and rebuilding than occurs in most places.[10] Also, the competitive nature of commercialism prompts owners of shops and other facilities to modernize and refashion frequently. According to Vladimir Krstic's research, the time between modifications of facades ranges from four months to two years, while extensive renovations or complete replacements occur every five to ten years.[11]

In general, as Krstic's research shows, the "annual degree of change in the urban [fabric within the numerous, and usually densely built commercial zones] is about 30%, including all modes of mutations ranging from facade reconstruction to newly built structures. ... Department stores and other large commercial buildings are the least changeable parts [in such urban areas]; their physical appearance is altered every thirty to fifty years, which, in most cases, [means] the destruction of the existing building and the erection of a new one."[12] Moreover, when properties are sold, too often only the land is traded, since the new owner will probably want to construct a new building. In fact some, like the owner of Ito's U House, actually have the building removed before selling the

land to make the deal more attractive to buyers. The "bubble economy" of the 1980s and early 1990s, accelerated all this, transforming Tokyo and other cities at a delirious rate. With the burst of the bubble, however, this did not cease; many small commercial complexes, such as Shin Takamatsu's Oxy Building in Kyoto (1991-94), have been torn down and converted into more profitable parking structures.

In Tokyo they demolish 12,339 sq.m. [132,644 sq.ft.] of buildings, and newly construct 62,861 sq.m. [675,755 sq.ft.] *daily*, while 455 units of new housing start every day [1993].
Tokyo Metropolis: Facts and Data.[13]

In other words, and perhaps not surprisingly, both the economy and the extraordinarily advanced nature of Japanese consumer society significantly affect the rapid life cycle of architecture and the changing cityscapes. As the second largest economic superpower, Japan has tremendous wealth, technological prowess, extensive investments, great research capabilities, highly skilled and dedicated workers, and a tremendous need and appetite for construction; it has the world's largest construction market accounting for more than 20% of the country's GNP and employing about 10% of its total labour force, while there is a severe shortage of construction workers.[14] No wonder, then, that entire cities, particularly Tokyo, seem constantly to be under construction; urban skylines are crowded with forests of cranes and rising or disappearing structures. Tokyo, in fact, is a "brand new" city. *Most* of its architecture has been constructed and/or reconstructed after the Second World War; according to a 1993 statistic, "more than 30% of all [its] structures...have been built since 1985."[15]

The historical growth of ... Japanese cities has not been a continuous flow; ... it has been always motivated by some catastrophic event.
Riichi Miyake, "Pursuit for Internal Microcosms"[16]

Ryoji Suzuki, Sagishima RING Guest House, Sagishima, Mihara, 1995. The three-storey building, the vacation lodge for the employees of a small company, is not only one of Suzuki's latest, but also most innovative designs epitomizing his long evolving neo-avantgarde architecture. Particularly striking is the articulation of its interior spaces as "gaps" that are dramatically yet poetically highlighted by intricate openings and lighting, as well as reflective surfaces, and enhanced by the dynamic elements of unique stairways and bridges, along with the skeletal matrix of the wooden structural system itself. They all join forces to conjure up a sense of phenomenal lightness and illusive ephemerality.

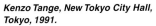

Kenzo Tange, New Tokyo City Hall, Tokyo, 1991.
The overall symmetrical scheme calls to mind the historic architectural model of European cathedrals, the spiritual centres of Western medieval cities. Tange's representation has been questioned by many as an appropriate expression of 20th-century Japan and Japanese urbanism, whose fluid and kaleidoscopic texture typically defies the emergence of a dominant order with a powerful centre.

Ruins resulting from Kobe Earthquake, January 17, 1995

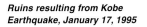

The Japanese Example **51**

As exemplified by the devastating Kobe earthquake of 1995 — in which more than 6,300 people perished and more than 100,200 houses were destroyed or damaged — Japanese cities are also subject to endless and unpredictable cycles of natural and other disasters and subsequent reconstructions.[17] An epitome of such phenomena, Tokyo "stands" as a city of repeated destructions as much as of rebuildings and revivals; perhaps no other city has been devastated and almost completely destroyed as often, given its relatively brief, four-hundred-year history.[18] Between 1603 and 1872 there were ninety-seven major conflagrations including catastrophic fires in 1657, 1682, 1720, and 1872; there were major earthquakes in 1855 and 1923; the fire bombings of the Second World War also razed the city. Yet it was rebuilt time and again, with speed and determination, although in these processes nearly all historic structures have been lost. Tokyo, like many Japanese cities, but unlike most Western ones, has no monuments; there is no "old town."

Perhaps as a result of its observation and interpretation of the subtle and not-so-subtle workings of *nature*, Japanese culture has evolved around the notion of *impermanence*. Regarding change and cyclical renewal, and specifically demolition and rebuilding, one has to remember that, according to religious rituals, Shinto shrines were rebuilt at regular intervals; today this unique custom, called *shikinen sengu* continues at Ise Jingu, which is torn down and rebuilt every twenty years, most recently in 1993.

Also according to ancient beliefs and rituals, upon the enthronement of a new Emperor, the entire capital of the country was dismantled, moved, and rebuilt in a different location (Naniwa, Asuka, Omi, Fujiwara, Kuni, Nagaoka, etc.), before first Nara (710-784) and then Kyoto (794-1868) became permanent capitals.

In medieval castle towns, various trade districts and numerous temple compounds were routinely relocated by landlords for various reasons, including the defence of the castle compound.[19]

Buddhist teachings — for instance, that there is "no permanence" and that "all things must pass" — have, in equally profound ways, conditioned the Japanese mentality towards the phenomena of change and the transitory nature of existence. Buddhism emphasizes the evanescence and insubstantiality of all things. Universal and immutable laws do not appeal to the Japanese. Nor does the logic of pure or autonomous identity; traditionally Japanese things have not been subjected to the process of individuation and objectification. The ultimate origin and destination of things in Japanese "metaphysics" is not an idealized perfect state (the "ideal"), but "nothingness" (*mu*), a plural void. For the Japanese, the heart or essence of everything is nothingness.

The present that we inhabit is nothing more than [a momentary] wedge in eternal nothingness.
Mitsuo Inoue, *Space in Japanese Architecture*[20]

More interested in circumstantial relationships and the concreteness of the interface between things than in the consistency of a well-defined, abstract system of wholes, the Japanese tend to apprehend things as events rather than as substance. This particular outlook has given the Japanese mentality a highly intuitive, situational, and paradoxical character; it has also shaped their ideas about the city or Japanese urban thought. Accordingly, in Japan, as opposed to most other, primarily Western cultures, there is no indigenous tradition of pursuing the notion of an "ideal city" or, in Henry D. Smith's words, "[there is] no tradition of using the city as a metaphor for utopian ideals."[21] Equally, there is no tradition of conceiving the city as a form of cosmic symbolism, and as an autonomous political system.[22] This mentality developed slowly, reaching its epitome during the Edo Period (1603-1868), but it has also been preserved to a remarkable extent even after the opening up of Japan to the West in the mid-nineteenth century.[23] Thus, although also changing, the long-cultivated understanding of human dwellings as only temporary

shelters, and cities, not unlike nature, as ephemeral realms, and, as such, elements of the "floating world" or *ukiyo* has remained a latent force in contemporary Japan.

If we compare the architecture of Western civilization to a museum, then Japanese architecture [can be likened to] a theatre.
Toyo Ito[24]

Today, along with the fast-running economy, exorbitant land prices, and ubiquitous commercialization, the most significant development shaping the cityscape is the shift from the once-dominant industrial or "hardware" technology to a new, invisible electronic or "software" technology that, like computer programmes, is run with "fuzzy logic." Since the late 1970s, architecture in Japan has been influenced increasingly by information and media technologies. Although capable of engaging the speculative mind, if used critically, these new technologies are predisposed to appeal to human emotions and desires; and they inspire an increased fascination with images, and with the sensual in architecture.

All of these phenomena, both historical and cultural, have resulted in the environment of late-capitalist society in Japan; an accelerated environment, an "urbanism in the fast lane." This is a radically volatile world with a "ruined map" — a place where one's sense of reality is profoundly challenged by the scenography of rapidly changing architecture or, conversely, a place where reality is now increasingly rendered as a dreamlike fiction. Indeed, Japanese urbanism has reached a stage in which much of the environment is produced by and consists of signs, images, and information. Tokyo, now a leading informational centre, has become the capital of the "Empire of Signs" as Roland Barthes perceptively called Japan.[25]

Tokyo has undergone many changes in physical appearance over the last century. The city, so decimated by World War II, has had to rebuild from

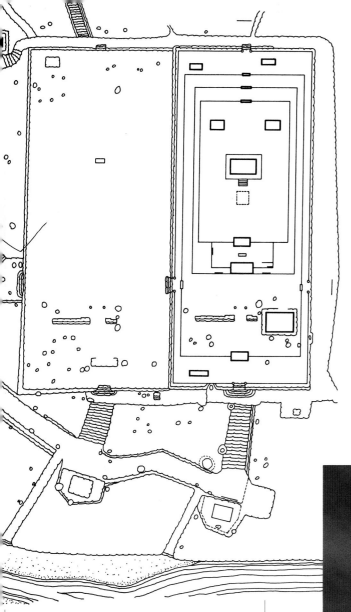

Fumihiko Maki: Spiral Building, Tokyo, 1985.
The large multi-storey cultural complex owned by the Wacoal Company is an infill building that displays only one facade to the busy Aoyama Avenue. This elevation is a collection of sophisticated elements, surfaces, and images that are collaged together in a rather unusual yet attractive manner, adding up to a largely fragmentary composition. Maki's design is rendered in highly polished aluminium, glass and other high-tech materials and structures, with references to Western classical, traditional Japanese and, more importantly, high-modernist architecture; it represents a new standard in regard to both architectural sensibility and the quality of public spaces. On the outside the facade spirals upwards, as does the long, ceremonial ramp inside the three-storey, top-lit atrium space that connects the first floor lobby, café and gallery with the second or mezzanine floor shops. All together, Maki's design is evocative of a quality of curious "lightness."

Ise Jingu Shinto Shrine compound, Ise, Mie Prefecture, 3rd century.
Dedicated to the Amaterasu Omikami Sun Goddess, the mythical ancestor of the Imperial family and, by extension, the Japanese nation, Ise is the most revered Shinto Shrine in Japan. According to ancient rituals of renewal, closely related to the Japanese observance of the cyclical changes of nature and the season of harvest, the entire shrine compound has been rebuilt at regular intervals from ancient times. Despite the tremendous expense involved, amounting to several million dollars, this custom of meticulous rebuilding (shikinen-sengu) in which once the new complex is finished the old one is demolished, continues in our time. Believed to date from the 3rd century AD, Ise is rebuilt every twenty years alternately on its two adjacent, identical sites. The latest, which is the sixty-first such identical rebuilding, took place in 1993.

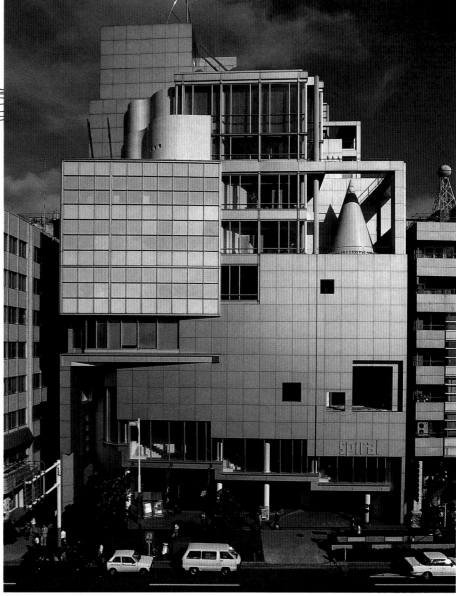

The Japanese Example

Shibuya Station Square, Tokyo.
One of Tokyo's busiest and most fashionable urban places, Shibuya is oriented to the large number of commuters changing trains here daily, and especially the fashion-conscious young people who flock to the area both day and night. In many ways Shibuya represents much of Tokyo and, by extension, the Japanese city: it is disordered, kaleidoscopic, fragmented, dense, with incongruous elements, but is both exhilarating and stimulating. It also reveals with poignant intensity the volatility and accelerated urban culture of the Japanese city; crowded by a forest of frequently changing signs, commercials, huge multi-storey-high TV screens, and neon lights, it displays a restlessness matched only by the busy lifestyles of Tokyoites. Not only the signs enveloping the archi-tecture beneath, but the buildings themselves are changing rapidly; in the past two decades almost all the surrounding structures have been demolished and rebuilt, including the two now under construction.

ashes. In its rebuilding it has become — perhaps it has returned to being — a city without heaviness. It was once a city of wood and paper; it has now become a city of concrete, steel, and glass. The feeling of lightness however remains.
Fumihiko Maki[26]

When opened to the West in 1853, Japan was essentially a feudal society. It launched a rapid programme of modernization and Japanese cities were refashioned according to Western models — Paris, London, Chicago, New York, etc. This resulted in tremendous changes in the urban landscape and urban life in a very short period. Traditional building was not considered a precedent to follow or preserve, and it was largely ignored until, interestingly, Western architects and historians drew the attention of the Japanese to the value of their own historic architecture.[27] In fact, the Japanese attitude towards their architectural past has always been ambivalent. The historian and theoretician Nyozekan Hasegawa, for example, argues that the importance of tradition in Japan "lies not so much in the preservation of the cultural properties of the past in their original form as in giving shape to contemporary culture; not in the retention of things as they were, but in the way certain ... qualities inherent in them live on in the contemporary culture."[28] In this regard it is revealing that "one private foundation in the city of Lübeck in Northern Germany spends the equivalent of about 60 million Yen [$500,000] a year on its own for the renovation of old buildings, while annual public financing for the urban renewal of the old medieval town core varied between 300 and 600 million Yen [$2,5 — $5 million] before the reunification of Germany. In Kyoto the total budget for more than thirty projects within the four preservation districts came to 60 million Yen in 1993."[29]

Tokyo is in many ways more enlightened than other cities. There is a process of dynamic change [at work here] ... and you have less hang-ups;

... the idea of a city that becomes like a museum, where you cannot pull down buildings simply because they are old is questionable. ... In that sense Tokyo is more liberated [than Western cities].
Sir Norman Foster, "A New Structural Expression for Tokyo"[30]

While Japan has succeeded in just about every respect — industrial production and economy, as well as architecture — in emulating and even surpassing its Western counterparts, its urban developments have never matched those of the West. Although Japanese cities have been rapidly modernized, this progress has consistently defied Western type urbanization. Tokyo, as much as other Japanese cities, has retained its pre-modern, Edo urban structure, its essence as an Oriental city, as well as its mental predisposition to favour the situational over the predetermined, to prefer integration without synthesis. This is apparent in the organization and quality of its built environment, which have remained largely unaffected by Western modernist urban design principles. Tokyo has continued to develop from its parts, piecemeal, according to "fuzzy logic," and thus the city has become a conglomeration of an endless variety of *patchwork*.

The architect and critic, Hajime Yatsuka has written: "Patchwork here means that there is no organic relationship between neighbouring elements such as streets and buildings, and that it is not possible to establish such a relationship. ... The tendency is to move from the texture to the patchwork, from the synthesized city to the city *sans organes*, from *la ville radieuse* to the patchwork city. ..."[31] Such a city is better defined by its events, human activities, fast and continuous change, and a penchant for novelty, than by the physical entity or material substance of its built fabric. Japanese architecture and urbanism, in the tradition of "ritual" building and rebuilding, constitute a culture of making-and-remaking rather than *making-and-holding*; what is preserved is thus the way of acting, the ritual of doing.

The city is not a work of art.
Arata Isozaki[32]

Until the mid to late 1970s, the "chaotic" processes of Japanese urbanization were disparaged by modernist architects and urbanists, as much as by modern society in general; the Japanese city was diagnosed as ugly, sick and incurable. With the advent of the post-industrial/ post-modern society and the age of information, however, this perspective began to change. Tokyo (and the Japanese city in general) was ready to rediscover itself in a new kind of urbanism, one as valid and as progressive as the models it wanted to emulate. The Japanese city began to measure itself on its own terms, not only in comparison with but also as opposed to classical and modern Western models. Beyond its many undeniable deficiencies and liabilities — congestion, high land prices, lack of natural landscapes, shortage of affordable housing — it now recognizes its many advantages and assets: energy, flexibility, innovation, spirit of community, etc. Indeed, against all odds, the Japanese city *works*, and works amazingly well. Recognition of this now comes as much, or more, from outside as from within Japan, and particularly from the West. Robert Venturi and Denise Scott Brown have commented: "What you see in contemporary Tokyo ... is an accommodation to and a celebration of the realities and tensions of our time; to the plurality of cultures promoted via global communication ...; and to the diversity and quantity of overlapping taste cultures. ... These complexities and contradictions and the resultant ambiguities lead to a richness of effect and a spirit that are the fate, and should be the ... art of our time."[33]

I believe [that today's] architecture must reflect the city called Tokyo.
Toyo Ito, "Shinjuku Simulated City"[34]

New developments in Japanese urbanism have elicited an astonishingly broad spectrum of interpretations and responses from Japanese designers. Debunking much of their previous aversions towards the city, architects have rediscovered its messy vitality, its flux, and its hidden, but still surviving Oriental traditions. In other words, these architects, despite divergent approaches, share one basic position: that heterogeneous, volatile, and chaotic urban conditions can be understood as a different kind of order rather than as anarchy, and can be the source not only of destructive forces but also of tremendously creative energies, and even of poetic inspiration. Indeed, the 1980s saw a radical paradigm shift in Japanese architecture and urbanism that has encouraged the appreciation and artistic exploration of the phenomenal and the ephemeral.

Although most architects expect their buildings to last for only a few years, they have been creating an architecture that, paradoxically, embodies futuristic qualities, and is realized with cutting-edge technologies and meticulous craftsmanship. Given the restlessness of the Japanese city, architectural experimentation and innovation are now not merely optional but almost unavoidable. And, as always in Japan, such experimentation occurs on the construction site, in the trial-and-error realm of reality, rather than, as with most other contemporary cultures, in academia or on the drawing board.

Urban Japan is the world's optimum urban laboratory: by definition experimental, it represents both the normal and ideal context in which architects should work. Here necessity has provoked a free-for-all reformulation of the evolving present; to non-Japanese eyes, a paroxysm of value-free juxtapositions, in which a kaleidoscope of random parts flourishes to the limits of possibility, with aggressive obliviousness to the whole. This accelerated drive trespasses on our reality and reveals new values.
Eleni Gigantes, "Lifestyle Superpower"[35]

After the Meiji Restoration of 1868, Tokyo became a laboratory for testing Western urban models, and continued as such for many years. In the wake of the explosive urban growth of the 1960s, the Metabolism movement revived this tradition of experimentation with much vigour and optimism. But in the movement's work and buildings one could identify early signs of a non-Western urbanism as well, especially insofar as the Metabolists' notions of change and interchangeability were derivative of tenets of Japanese Buddhism and traditional urbanism. Metabolist architects such as Kiyonori Kikutake and Kisho Kurokawa recognized that certain elements in the built environment wear out or, because of technological progress, become obsolete much faster than others and hence the need to replace them would be more frequent. But Kenzo Tange and the Metabolists who relied on industrial technology in their architecture and urban schemes could not reconcile the fact that the model of change they advocated was implicated in the growing consumerism of Japanese society, in the relentless cycles of fashion, and in entertainment, all of which they, as modernists, criticized and wished to avoid. And the megastructural architecture they produced turned out to be, for the most part, as heavy, monumental, and inflexible as the prevailing modern Western urban models they sought to overhaul. In the end, this architecture, as best exemplified by Tange's Festival Plaza at the Osaka Expo 1970, also shifted towards entertainment.

Kojeve observed after a trip to Japan that ... Japan seemed to offer the spectacle of a society that had for nearly three centuries "experienced life at the 'end of History.'"
Masao Miyoshi and Harry D. Harootunian. *Postmodernism and Japan*[36]

Emerging rapidly in the 1970s and coming of age — a "golden age" — with the "bubble economy" of the 1980s, the "new wave" of Japanese architecture, instead of striving for monumental permanence, began to foster new "urban sensibilities" to engage and thrive on the city's dynamics and to probe the notion of impermanence in architecture. Contemporary design in Japan is characterized by a phenomenal lightness, surface, fragmentation, and dissolution, often with a "ruinous" quality, a sense of temporality, imageability, sensuousness, and, finally, a spectacular phenomenalism — all attributes of the ephemeral; combined with new interpretations of nature and the new software technologies, it favours ambiguity, transparency, and perceptual instability with an implicit indeterminacy of meaning.

Ito, one of the architects most aware of the predicament of fast-changing conditions and flux of the Japanese city, has concluded that "the residents of Tokyo can ... be compared to [urban] nomads wandering in artificial forests," for whom "a tent would suffice" as shelter.[37] He has borrowed the concept of "nomadism" from Gilles Deleuze and Felix Guattari who, in *Mille Plateaux*, depict the beginning of a new migratory state in our late capitalist society. Accordingly, many of his designs, including the Silver Hut (1984), the Nomad Restaurant (1986-89), and the Yatsushiro Municipal Museum (1991), appear to be only temporary structures; light and insubstantial, they are intended to defy any sense of monumentality. Itsuko Hasegawa's concept of "architecture as second nature" and Kazunari Sakamoto's "architecture as environment rather than as object" refer to similar intentions with similar results. The Shonandai Cultural Centre (1991) by Hasegawa, Sakamoto's Hoshida Common City Housing (1993), as well as projects by Riken Yamamoto, such as the Rotunda (1987) and Hamlet (1988), are virtual high-tech camps which, by way of their unique use of the least amount of material — thin metal sheeting, canvas, Teflon fibre and other screens — appear to occupy the borderland between concrete reality and the freedom of a dream.

[Here] architecture is proposed as a field of exploration of untold and unforeseen dimensions found in the experiential and imaginative limitlessness of time, space, and matter. ... Simultaneously the whole idea of corporeality appears redefined in a fascinating way when the intensity of

Toyo Ito, Yatsushiro Municipal Museum, Yatsushiro, Kumamoto Prefecture, 1991. Contrary to established, often monumental models of museum architecture, Ito has articulated his design with readily available and ordinary industrial materials, and a design sensibility that suggests elusive lightness and the feeling of temporality.

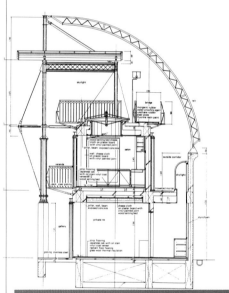

*Riken Yamamoto, "Hamlet"
Residential Complex, Tokyo, 1988*

*Itsuko Hasegawa: Sumida Culture Factory, Tokyo, 1994.
Located in a densely built, traditional working-class area of Tokyo, Hasegawa's building, shaped and finished largely with metallic materials, perforated aluminium, and layers of translucent screens, intends to create a metaphysical townscape for the Sumida district. Around a small inner plaza, three volumes accommodate assembly and communication spaces, a hall, and a planetarium; an information centre and a library; and study rooms, offices, and counselling rooms for children. The three parts are connected by bridges. Like most of Hasegawa's recent architecture, this design is characterized by an almost immaterial definition of architectural spaces.*

Kazunari Sakamoto, Hoshida Common City Housing, Katano, Osaka Prefecture, 1994. Sakamoto's 112 houses have a steel frame reinforced concrete structure, corrugated metallic sheets on most walls and curving, lightweight metallic roofs over steel frames that seem to float above the well-lit spaces of the living areas below. Areas in between buildings are attractively landscaped, and residential units with carefully focused windows open onto small interconnected parks. A small community centre, with open terraces, a waterfall, and other facilities, mostly under Teflon fibre tent structures stretched over a vaulted metallic frame, is also included. Sakamoto's straightforward but sensitive articulation of the small buildings, along with the materials and structures used make his architecture representative of a new "industrial vernacular."

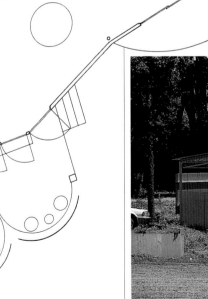

Kazuo Sejima, Platform House #2, Yamanashi Prefecture

architecture's material existence is achieved in the moment of its physical abstraction and pending disappearance with the purpose not to concretise the object itself but create a perceptual mirage.
Vladimir Krstic, "Stillness of Hyperreality: The In(de)finite City"[38]

Recognizing that the role of architecture is to *envelop* increasingly elusive phenomena, much of the new architecture is comprised of little material substance. Kazuyo Sejima's Platform Houses, for example, are as close to an immaterial evocation of architecture as possible; they are merely stages — platforms — for "unlimited" or unpredictable human action. Even Tadao Ando, the architect of reinforced concrete, has built several "light" structures. The Karaza Temporary Theatre (1987) and, particularly, the second Tea House in Oyodo (1988-93), among others, are outstanding examples of an "architecture of the ephemeral;" incorporating only a thin steel frame, glass floor and canopy, and roll-up "walls" of synthetic fabric screens, the latter was perched on the rooftop ridge of a two-storey building in a crowded part of Osaka. This spectacular small piece of architecture reacted with the energy of the surrounding city even as it remained aloof from the urban jumble below; like an evanescent Japanese flower arrangement or *ikebana*, it lasted only a short while.

The "essence" of these light constructions is not only related to natural, human, and urban phenomena, but also in effect evoked by them. In these structures one can observe the gradual "dissipation" of opacity, and so, also the impending or hypothetical disappearance of Architecture itself. Appearing as temporary shelters, often hardly more than a thin and "floating" membrane of roof, many recent works by Toyo Ito, Kazuyo Sejima, Itsuko Hasegawa, Kazunari Sakamoto, Hiroshi Hara, Riken Yamamoto, Fumihiko Maki, and others, conjure up ephemerality. This architecture, aspiring to evoke the perceptual impermanence of building, has brought about a new "industrial vernacular," on the

one hand, and a new kind of "imminent space," on the other.

The aesthetic that [the Japanese] cityscape generates is one that favours fluctuations, fluidity, and lightness; it suggests the discovery of a new perceptual order.
Fumihiko Maki, "City Image, Materiality"[39]

Also inspired by the ephemerality of the information society, and especially by its manifestations in the Japanese city, Fumihiko Maki's progressively "dematerialized" and increasingly ambiguous architecture reveals not only a highly sophisticated fragmentary quality, but also a transcendental lightness. Talking about the shapes of his recent work, he often uses the analogy of "cloud-like" formations. "An order in which the relationship of the parts to the whole is systematic might be labelled a 'clock,' and a condition in which the parts and the whole are in an *unstable* equilibrium, might be labeled a 'cloud'. ... [Here] the whole remains *indeterminate* and cloudlike."[40]

[The] ephemeral, taken in a positive sense, [does not necessarily] mean that the architecture is short-lived, but that new meanings are perpetually emerging.
Koji Taki, "Towards an open text: On the work and thoughts of Toyo Ito."[41]

Striving for such a formal instability or for a hypothetical condition of "no form," is also evident in Ito's so-called "wind architecture," which he has combined with his architecture of "urban nomads." In the wind-blown tents of nomads there is no distinction between formation and deformation — between form and no form. To achieve such a condition, Ito often relies on computer or media technologies, as exemplified by the Tower of the Winds (1986) in Yokohama; the tower, like a huge electronic gauge with thousands of flickering lights, has virtually no permanent image: it is ceaselessly generated by the velocity and direction of the wind, the surrounding

sound level, and the passing of time. With similar goals, he has recently begun to design his projects — such as the Mediatheque, a library now under construction in Sendai — as complex "spaces of flows" and his urban architecture as "the city as a garden of microchips." In like fashion, Hiroshi Hara interprets and "designs" much of his architecture as an "electronic garden."[42]

If I were to leave my imprint on earth I would chose it to be, not in the form of a solid, monumental building — that is the way of the past — but in the ruins of something that has been blasted to pieces and blotted out.
Arata Isozaki, in an Interview with *Playboy.*[43]

One more aspect of the architecture of the ephemeral must be mentioned. In addition to responding to prevailing urban conditions, and thus cultivating a sentiment for anti-monumental architecture, architects in Japan are keenly aware of the possibility of unpredictable catastrophes, such as that experienced recently in Kobe. Thus, as Riichi Miyake wrote, "[In Japan] the will to build a city and to construct a building has been constantly next to the reality of destruction and included an impulse to destroy the unified whole."[44] With an almost zen-like consciousness, most designers know intuitively that every act of construction, in one way or another, is also an act of destruction, and vice versa. This understanding is poignantly spelled out by Arata Isozaki in his witty essay, "City Demolition Industry Inc."[45] Japanese architecture often makes no clear distinction between construction and demolition, the completed and the ruined. Many new designs, as if foretelling some impending "disaster," seem to reveal signs of ruins. The qualities of ruin are, of course, closely related to those of fragmentation, dissolution, scenography, etc.

[In the Japanese view, also] critical consciousness appears immaterial ... before such a visible and tangible [economic] success.

Hiroshi Hara, "Modal Space of Consciousness"
Exhibition Installation, Walker Art Center, USA,
1986.
This multi-layered structural model is composed
of twenty electronically programmed illuminated
robots, each of which is formed by a plexiglass
sandwich. Each robot functions as a "Light
Instrument" and together they form an orchestra
whose performance is a sequence of 8192
measures. Hara's intention is to offer a "look into
one's own consciousness."

Masao Miyoshi and Harry D. Harootunian, *Postmodernism and Japan*[46]

On the other hand, in the accelerated and simulated world of the Japanese city, despite the individual efforts of many architects, conditions do not favour a well-definable critical practice. In the "age of the ephemeral" only the slightest distinction exists between criticism and conformism. In other words, a critical practice in architecture tends to be implicated or absorbed in the very processes it intends to oppose or at least constrain. Maintaining a critical position in Japan means pursuing a practice that is at odds with technological domination, rampant consumerism, and empty image making, and yet acknowledging their *modus operandi* as the last viable alternative for architectural and perhaps also urban renewal.

This much is clear in the words of Toyo Ito: "I often use the word 'floating' not only to describe a lightness I want to achieve in architecture, but also to express a belief that our lives are losing touch with reality. All of life is becoming a pseudo-experience. This trend is being encouraged by the consumer society, and architecture itself is rapidly becoming more image — or consumption — oriented. This is a matter of grave concern to the architect yet, at the same time, architecture today must be made to relate to this situation. This is the contradiction we are confronted with." But he continues: "I do not want merely to reject this state of affairs; instead, I want to enter into this situation a bit further and to confirm what sort of architecture is possible (within it)."[47] His concept of "nomadism," for example, is advanced in opposition to

what is sedentary, and stable, and which determines order, knowledge and occupation. Nomadism, says the architect Lynne Breslin, rejects "Western metaphysics based on authority and complicity with the state ... in favour of the forces of nature, change and the open-ended traversing of space."[48]

[On the other hand] the Japanese too often and too readily yield to the pressure for novelty and the promise of the new.
Botond Bognar. *World Cities: Tokyo*[49]

Yet, much of the work of these architects can be criticized, as was the activity of the 17th-century *sukiya* masters, for example, who were accused of overindulgence in the aesthetics of architecture as a form of political escapism. However, to quote Vladimir Krstic again: "if the alternative to their architecture [of the ephemeral], relative to the problematic of the Japanese city, is a looming corporate totalitarianism as evidenced by projects like Tange's New Tokyo City Hall complex [1991], then not only does the choice become self-evident, but at the same time the work of [these architects also] attains an important political perspective."[50] In this sense, then, Japanese architects, realizing that they cannot isolate themselves from society, have throughout the years shown an increasing capacity not only to deal with the excessively complex and contradictory conditions advanced by the society in which they operate, but also to combine innovative solutions with critical gestures and poetic poignancy.

Inspired by new social and urban developments, and facilitated by new materials,

structures, and technologies, the evolving new design paradigm can evoke and construct "architecture" with an almost immaterial lightness and transparency; here lightness and transparency as metaphors are the manifestations of a new understanding of a world in flux, whose paradoxical order of "creative chaos" can be approached only with a radically new "modal consciousness" unfettered by conservative, perspectival conceptions of the world. Günter Nitschke put it this way: "In 'A Garden of Microchips,' a metaphor used by Toyo Ito, or in 'Architecture as Second Nature,' one used by Itsuko Hasegawa, or in 'Electronics Garden,' one used by Hiroshi Hara in a recent urban design competition, one finds no more reference to the by now redundant imagery of traditional urban aesthetics, Western or Eastern, of High-Culture or of *Gemütlichkeit*. It is not merely an expansion of human consciousness we encounter in these discourses and creations; it is an intensification of it, which suggests an ever greater sense of transparency and sense of wholeness both in the contemplation and in the making of our world and of ourselves. These visions herald the dawn of an aperspectival world."[51]

In Japan today we find an ephemerality which, at its best, can paradoxically yield "lasting" or enduring achievements in urban as well as architectural design — regardless of how short their material existence may turn out to be. Therefore, as Vittorio Gregotti has said, "...Japan will undoubtedly remain a subject of close attention, for the importance which its *mutations* will have for all architectural culture in the years to come."[52]

Kazunari Sakamoto, House F, Tokyo, 1988

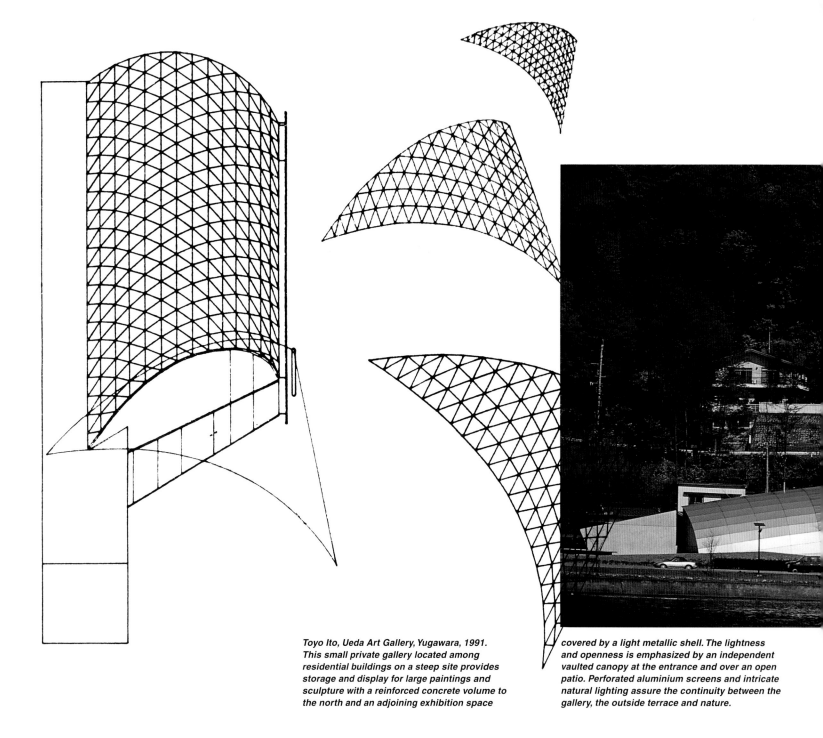

Toyo Ito, Ueda Art Gallery, Yugawara, 1991. This small private gallery located among residential buildings on a steep site provides storage and display for large paintings and sculpture with a reinforced concrete volume to the north and an adjoining exhibition space

covered by a light metallic shell. The lightness and openness is emphasized by an independent vaulted canopy at the entrance and over an open patio. Perforated aluminium screens and intricate natural lighting assure the continuity between the gallery, the outside terrace and nature.

Notes:

1 Ryoji Suzuki, "Absolute Scene Tokyo 1987" in B. Bognar, *World Cities: Tokyo*, London: Academy Editions, 1997. p. 183.

2 Igasi de Solá-Morales. *Differences*. Quoted in the *Harvard Design Magazine*, Fall 1997, p.2.

3 John Thackara. "In Tokyo they shimmer, chatter and vanish" *The Independent* (London) Wednesday 25 September 1991, in the Architecture section on the Japanese exhibition T-Zone in The Collection Gallery, London. 25 September-20 October 1991, p.12).

4 The central part, including the lobby, of the Hotel was rebuilt in the village museum of Meiji-mura, north of Nagoya, in 1985 at a cost of millions of dollars.

5 These conversations took place in the respective Tokyo offices of Ito and Takeyama, between the architects and myself during May 1997. About his U House Ito has eventually written: "[Since the completion of the White U House in 1976] the...environment has transformed dramatically and the lifestyles of the occupants have changed....After 20 years, the house had finished its task. After further discussion, [the resident owners] decided that they did not want others to live there, so they chose to demolish it. I felt the same way and agreed with their decision." (T. Ito, "White U," *ANY* #19/20, 1997, p.20/10)

6 Vittorio Gregotti, "Japan: a dis-oriented modernity." in *Japan: a dis-oriented modernity*, Special issue of *Casabella*. Nos. 608-609. (January-February) 1994, p.113. (Emphasis by B. Bognar)

7 Japan is an island country of 146,000 square miles and 125 million people. With high mountains and volcanoes occupying the majority of its territory, less than 30% of it remains for habitation, agriculture, and everything else.

8 Quoted in the *Japan Almanac 1993*. Tokyo: Asahi Shimbunsha, 1992. p.186 (1 square meter - ¥33,500,00; US$1=¥135.

9 Judith Connor Greer. "Tokyo in Transition." *Japan: An Illustrated Encyclopedia*. Tokyo: Kodansha, 1993. p. 1592.

10 However in absolute cost, expressed in dollars, construction is somewhat more expensive in Japan than in the United States.

11 Vladimir Krstic "A Life Act and Urban Scenography: Supraphysical Concept of Urban Form in the Core of the Japanese City." Master Thesis at Kyoto University c. 1985, p.44.

12 Ibid, pp.44-45

13 *Tokyo Metropolis: Facts and Data*. Tokyo: Tokyo Metropolitan Government, 1994, p.16.

14 *Japan: An Illustrated Encyclopedia*. Op. cit. 5, p. 235., and *Japan Almanac 1997*. Tokyo: Asahi Shimbunsha, 1996, p.159.

15 Ichiro Suzuki and Scott M. Gold, "Collective Housing: Typologies in Evolution," in *Japan: a dis-oriented modernism*, Special issue of *Casabella* Nos 608-609, Jan/Feb. 1994, p.119.

16 Riichi Miyake. "Pursuit for Internal Microcosms." *The Japan Architect*. January 1987, p. 6.

17 *Japan Almanac 1997*, Op. cit.12, p. 236

18 Tokyo's predecessor, Edo was in effect established by the shogun Tokugawa Ieyasu (1543-1616) in the late sixteenth century.

19 Traditional architecture was of wood construction which allowed for "easy" dismantling and reassembling. However, in case of the Ise Shrine (as with all Shinto Shrines before), after the completion of the new compound on an adjacent and identical site, and at a cost of millions of dollars, the old one is pulled down.

20 Mitsuo Inoue. *Space in Japanese Architecture*. H. Watanabe, trans. New York and Tokyo: Weatherhill, 1985. p.171.

21 Henry D. Smith II, "Tokyo as an Idea: An Exploration of Japanese Urban Thought until 1945" in *Journal of Japanese Studies*, 4/1 (Winter '78), p.45.

22 The two ancient Japanese capitals Heijo-kyo (Nara) and Heian-kyo (Kyoto) were, patterned along Chinese models, and as such were originally reflective of the Chinese cosmic view. Nevertheless, the Japanese, as soon as they received these urban concepts and forms, deviated from them substantially. In other words, the cosmic relation between the city and an abstract cosmos was not sustained. Although, the Japanese city, having been a form of mediation between humans and nature, and nature being inhabited by the myriads of *kami* for the Japanese, was a link between the world of humans and those of "gods" or spirits. For further details, see Henry D. Smith II, "Tokyo as an Idea: An Exploration of Japanese Urban Thought Until 1945," ibid.

23 Botond Bognar, "The Place of No-thingness: the Japanese House and the Oriental World Views of the Japanese." in J-P. Bourdier and N. Alsayyad (eds). *Dwellings, Settlements and Tradition*. Lanham, MD. University Press of America, 1989. p.201.

24 Toyo Ito in an interview with Sophie Roulet and Sophie Soulie, entitled "Towards a post-ephemeral architecture," in Sophie Roulet and Sophie Soulie (eds.). *Toyo Ito*. Paris: Editions

Toyo Ito, Shimosuwa Municipal Museum, Shimosuwa, Nagano Prefecture, 1993.
The site of the museum parallels the shore line of Suwa Lake which is to the south. The volume housing the exhibition spaces follows this curving, narrow but more than 100m long site. The entire design is dominated by the "arched" and double bent form of the unusually long

building. The shape is provided by bent steel frames 3m apart and thin metal plates which all together draw an arc in both section and elevation adding up to a three dimensional surface. From afar it resembles a ship turned upside down floating on the lake or, alternatively, it can be seen as a huge wave emerging from the water. To emphasize the dynamics and floating

quality of this shell structure, its surface is covered by an independent 3mm aluminium membrane; when bouncing back the changing daylight or the lights of the night, the building is turned into a glowing arch; it appears as a mirage.

Moniteur, 1991, p.105.

25 Roland Barthes. *Empire of Signs*. Richard Howard, trans. New York: Hill and Wang, 1982, p. 30.

26 Fumihiko Maki, "The Roof at Fujisawa," *Perspecta* No 24, (1988), p. 120.

27 Among these foreigners were the British Josiah Conder, the American Frank Lloyd Wright, the German Bruno Taut, and Walter Gropius, to mention only the better known ones; but there were many others, non-architects too, who all, coming to Japan at various times, "discovered" traditional Japanese architecture and gardens, and, while forwarding their own ideologies in design, introduced them enthusiastically in their works, built and written, to the world. They were also instrumental in directing the attention of the Japanese to their built heritage.

28 Nyozekan Hasegawa. *The Japanese Character*. John Bestor, trans. Tokyo: Kodansha International, 1965. pp.101-102.

29 Quoted in Uta Hohn, "Townscape preservation in Japanese urban planning," in *Town Planning Review, TPR* 68 (2), 1997. p.233.

30 Norman Foster. "A New Structural Expression for Tokyo," *The Japan Architect* 3-1991. p147.

31 Hajime Yatsuka. "An Architecture Floating on the Sea of Signs," in B. Bognar. *The New Japanese Architecture*. New York: Rizzoli, 1990, p.39.

32 Arata Isozaki is quoted in Yatsuka Hajime, "Between West and East — Part III," *Telescope* #8. Tokyo: Autumn 1992, p.87.

33 Robert Venturi and Denise Scott Brown, "Architecture as

Elemental Shelter, The City as Valid Decon," in *Architectural Design Profile 94. New Museums,* 1991, p. 13.

34 Toyo Ito, "Shinjuku Simulated City," in *The Japan Architect*, 3/1991, p. 51.

35 Eleni Gigantes, "Lifestyle Superpower: Urban Japan as Laboratory of the Limits of Reality." *Telescope.* Winter 1993, p165.

36 Masao Miyoshi and Harry D. Harootunian. *Postmodernism and Japan*. Durham, N.C.: Duke University Press, 1989, p.XII-XIII.

37 Toyo Ito in an Interview with Sophie Roulet and Sophie Soulie, entitled "Towards a post-ephemeral architecture," in Sophie Roulet and Sophie Soulie (eds.). *Toyo Ito.* Paris: Editions Moniteur, 1991, pp. 96 & 97.

38 Vladimir Krstic. "Stillness of Hyperreality: The In(de)finite City," in *Japanese Architecture II, Architectural Design* Profile No.99 (1992), p. 26.

39 Fumihiko Maki. "City Image, Materiality" in Serge Salat with Françoise Labbe. *Fumihiko Maki: An Aesthetic of Fragmentation.* New York: Rizzoli, 1988, p. 8.

40 Fumihiko Maki, "City Image, Materiality." Ibid, pp.10 & 11. (emphasis by B. Bognar)

41 Koji Taki. "Towards an open text: On the work and thoughts of Toyo Ito." in Sophie Roulet and Sophie Soulie (eds.). *Toyo Ito.* Paris: Editions Moniteur, 1991, p. 17.

42 Toyo Ito in *JA Library 2, The Japan Architect*, Summer 1993; *Arch+ 123*, September 1994; and Hiroshi Hara in *GA Japan* Environmental Design 13, March/April 1995

43 Arata Isozaki, in an 1984 interview in the Japanese edition

of *PLAYBOY*, quoted in Peter Popham, *Tokyo: The city at the End of the World.* (Tokyo: Kodansha International, 1985), 34.

44 Riichi Miyake. "Pursuit for Internal Microcosms." Op. cit. 17, p. 6.

45 Arata Isozaki. "City Demolition Industry Inc." in K. Frampton (ed.). *A New Wave of Japanese Architecture.* Catalog 10. New York: IAUS, 1978, p.51.

46 Masao Miyoshi and Harry D. Harootunian (eds.). *Postmodernism and Japan.* Op. cit. 36, p.XI.

47 Toyo Ito, "Shinjuku Simulated City." Op. cit. 30.

48 Lynne Breslin, "From the Savage to the Nomad," in B. Bognar (ed.), *Japanese Architecture, Architectural Design Profile 73, Vol. 58, No 5/6 1988,* p. 30.

49 Botond Bognar. *World Cities: Tokyo.* London: Academy Editions, 1997. p.34.

50 Vladimir Krstic, "Stillness of Hyperreality: The In(de)finite City" in B . Bognar (ed.), *Japanese Architecture II, AD Profile* No.99, 1992. p.26.

51 Günter Nitschke, "From Ambiguity to Transparency. Unperspective, perspective, and aperspective paradigm of space" in Japan Today. *Louisiana Revy* Vol.35, No.3, June 1995, (no pagination).

52 Vittorio Gregotti, "Japan: a dis-oriented modernity," Op. cit, 2. p.113. (emphasis by B. Bognar)

This article is a revised version of "What Goes Up, Must Come Down" which appeared in the Harvard Design Magazine, Fall 1997. All photographs by the author.

Broadcast.

TECHNICIAN 6 counts windows, verifying
use. TECHNICIAN stops. Searches.

LEBBEUS WOODS

Siteline Vienna, A project for the measurement of cultural differences, Summer 1998

SITELINE VIENNA (SLV) is a project devoted to the examination of the nation-state in the manufacture and control of culture in light of recent technological developments and the emergence of a new world order.

The last two decades have witnessed a fundamental restructuring of global power along economic, political and cultural lines. While the first two elements have received considerable attention and analysis, the role of culture in this restructuring has been largely overlooked or misunderstood.

Being both in the centre and on the periphery of European culture, Vienna provides the ideal setting for an enquiry into the economic and political functions of culture on the brink of a new millennium.

A union of European nation-states carries significant repercussions for its peoples. Divested of its currency, its rivalries, and in many ways its history, a nation-state must radically rethink its identity. This cannot occur without a major shift in consciousness.

SLV will measure the ways this occurs in local and global terms.

The project has three basic components:

1. A sequence of INSTRUMENT STATIONS, constructed on sites located on a straight line drawn between the Austrian Museum of Applied Art (MAK) and the Austrian Parliament building – a line crossing the historic centre of Vienna; their purpose is the measurement of the cultural differences that exist in Vienna's First District.

The line is drawn six to eight metres above street level in order to avoid interference with pedestrian and vehicular traffic; hence, the basic architectural task is the creation of

inhabitable space in mid-air, the hitherto unoccupied space between the buildings and above the street. This task is made more complex by the temporary nature of the instrument stations, which cannot, therefore, be supported by structural elements fixed to the adjacent buildings.

2. A team of TECHNICIANS, who will inhabit the instrument stations.

Each station is inhabited by one or more Technicians conducting various cultural measurements. Their exact function will be determined by a vocabulary of performance elements: speech, movement, routinized behaviour.

Different stations will examine the different aspects of daily life as they are evident in the culturally diverse sites (see the map of the First District).

3. A CENTRAL STATION, located in the front exhibition gallery of the MAK, will become an office serving as a headquarters, a press/public relations bureau, and a communications centre.

Because of recent budget cuts, the Museum has had to give up the former "art exhibition" function of this gallery space; and it has turned it over to SLV operations.

The former gallery space is divided into three parts, each of which is visible from the other two:

(a) a waiting room, which the public is free to enter; both sitting and standing room is available, as well as free brochures about the SLV operation;

(b) a public relations section (similar to the "customer service" areas in banks, which can be entered only by appointment (which is secured by written application in the waiting

Site: 1st District
Vienna, Austria

Collaborative partner: Austrian
Museum of Applied Art (MAK)
Peter Noever, Director

Construction date: Summer, 1998

Concept and design: LEBBEUS
WOODS ARBEITSGEMEINSCHAFT
WIEN
Lebbeus Woods and Dwayne
Oyler (project design)
Ekkehard Rehfeld (project
architect)

Drawings: Lebbeus Woods

Models: Dwayne Oyler

Photography: Lebbeus Woods and
Dwayne Oyler

OPPOSITE: SLV, Station 01
Stubenring 5 (MAK)

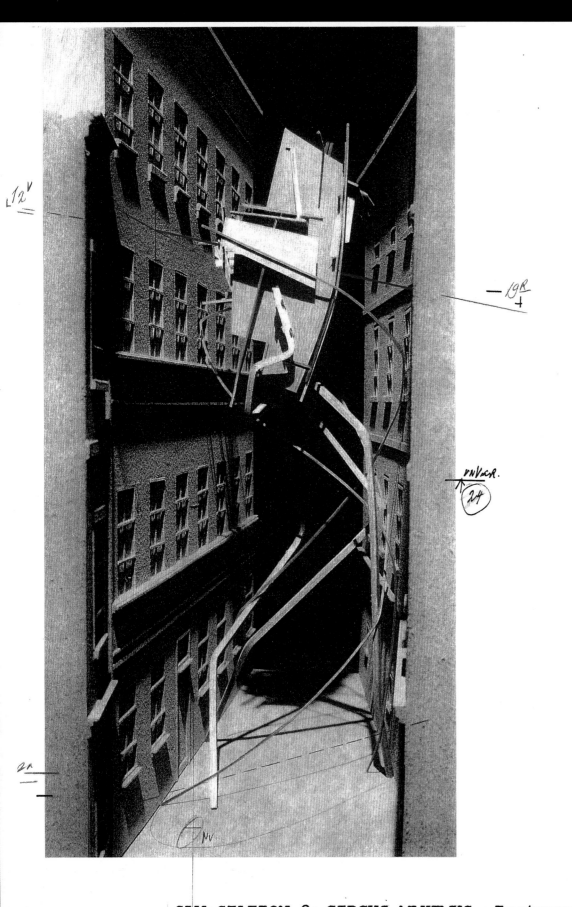

SLV:STATION 2: CIRCUS MAXIMUS. Instrument
blue-red of television _____. Blur of lat
_____. TECHNICIAN 2A motionless,
Break. Announcement for Viennese personal
TECHNICIAN 2A responds. Articulates. In p

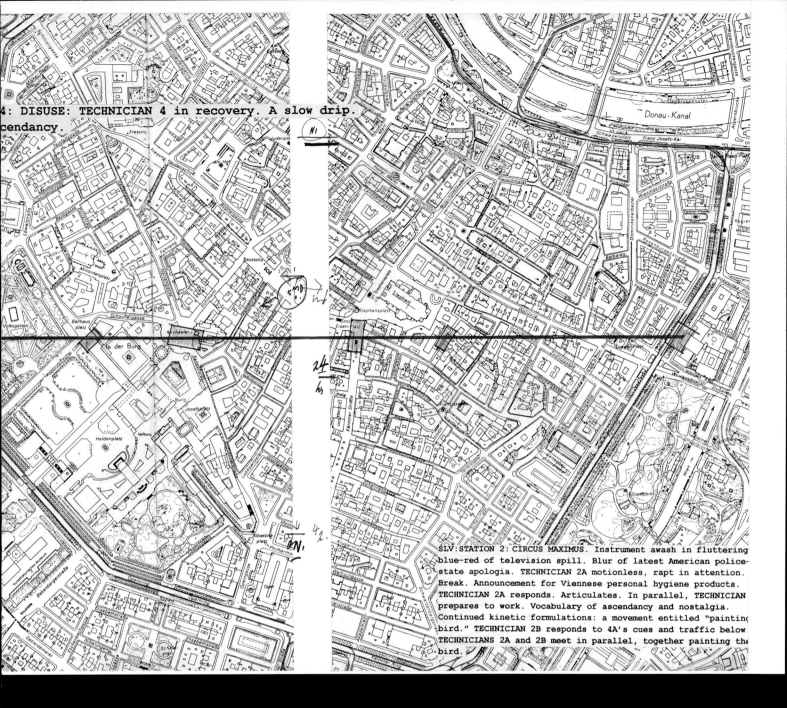

4: DISUSE: TECHNICIAN 4 in recovery. A slow drip.
cendancy.

SLV:STATION 2: CIRCUS MAXIMUS. Instrument awash in fluttering
blue-red of television spill. Blur of latest American police-
state apologia. TECHNICIAN 2A motionless, rapt in attention.
Break. Announcement for Viennese personal hygiene products.
TECHNICIAN 2A responds. Articulates. In parallel, TECHNICIAN
prepares to work. Vocabulary of ascendancy and nostalgia.
Continued kinetic formulations: a movement entitled "painting
bird." TECHNICIAN 2B responds to 4A's cues and traffic below
TECHNICIANS 2A and 2B meet in parallel, together painting the
bird.

LEFT: SLV Station 2, Blutgasse
ABOVE: SLV instrument stations 1st District, Vienna

room), and addresses any special questions or problems arising from the SLV operations; and

(c) the command centre, which consists of staff and equipment overseeing the day-to-day SLV operations as well as a media area for press announcements and presentations; this is not directly accessible to the public, but only to certified, invited members of the press.

The SLV is an agency identified only by the symbol or logo of a black Greek cross (+), the logotype SLV, and the uniforms of its Staff and Technicians.

SLV is an all-purpose acronym. Example: Synergistics, Energy, Viability.

The Director of Operations of SLV confers regularly with the Director of the MAK to discuss policy and to plan for its development.

As the SLV logo in all its manifestations begins to appear throughout the Museum, it is clear that SLV operations will expand.

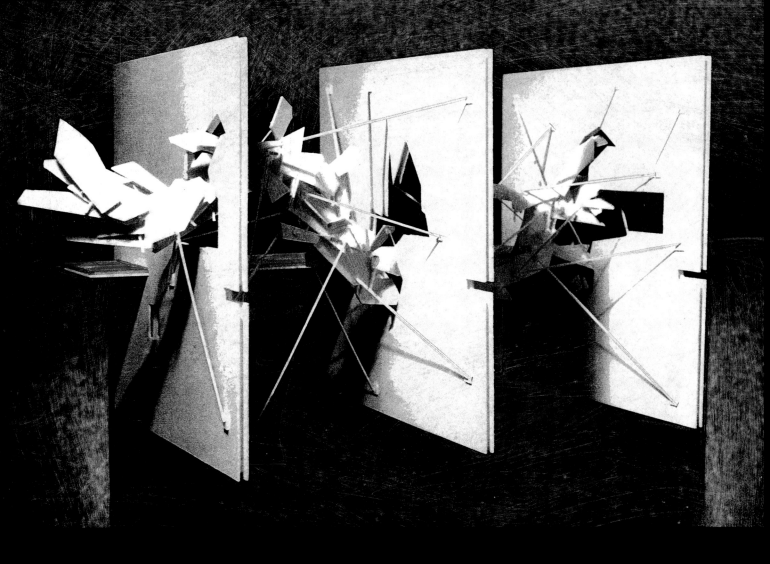

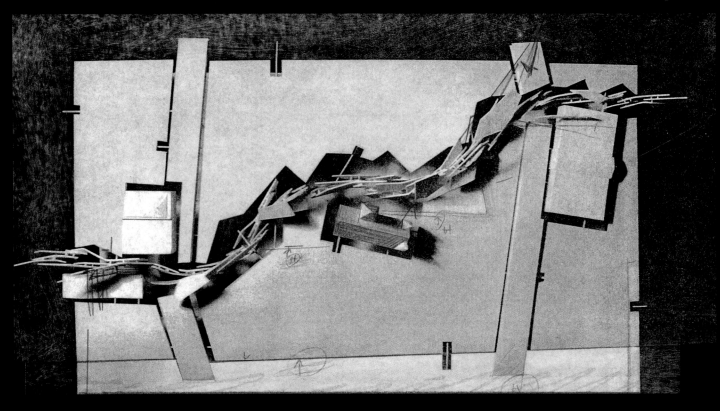

ABOVE: SLV, Station 01 Stubenring 5 (MAK); BELOW: SLV, Conceptual study, Stefansdom

SLV: Conceptual study Stefansdom

JUMP CUTS

Permanent installation at United Artists
Cineplex Theater, San Jose, 1995

The traditional theatre "marquee" en-
croached into the civic space of the sidewalk
to announce an event in a mute space
beyond: the marquee was always a form of
urban seduction. *Jump Cuts* interprets the

contemporary as a sculptural, electronic and
video apparatus that broadcast images and
texts, both informational and contempla-
tive, to the street.

Adding to the atmosphere of spectacle
already at play in the recently built United
Artists theatre, the installation teases visual
accessibility into the glazed lobby by flip-
ping the building inside-out and back,
electronically. An armature appended to the
theatre's north facade supports twelve liquid
crystal panels which phase between transparent surfaces and translucent projection
screens. Twelve video projectors,
cantilevered into the interior, sequence
direct feed from a series of live cameras
positioned over the escalators which scan
bodies in plan and elevation, movie trailers
advertising present films, and *unmediated*
views through the glass wall.

This marquee seduces by toggling between visual access and denial, by equating
the spectacle of movies with the spectacle of
moving bodies on parade circulating
through the lobby; and by exchanging live
bodies in deep space seen through the
curtain wall with the their live video counterparts – flattened, reconfigured, and
broadcast to the street.

Diller+Scofidio

Installations

SOFT SELL

*Temporary video installation at entrance to the
Rialto (porno theatre), 42nd Street, New York*

42nd Street has always been defined by
reversible values, an "unsightly" tourist sight
in which the friction between decadence
and delight produces a meeting ground of
conflicting patronage. It's a marketplace in
which successive forms of *currency* have
continually supplanted one another: high
society entertainment gave way to cabaret
society, which gave way to the movie
industry, then to popular amusements, to
commercial sex and illicit drugs and, most
recently, to fashionable merchandise and
family entertainment. Using two familiar
mechanisms of seduction, the female mouth
(here, reciting a chain of improbable solicita-
tions to passersby) and the peep show (here,
luring viewers from the street to look
through small liquid crystal openings to an
improbable scene inside the theatre), *Soft
Sell* offers a critical look at the production
of desire.

COLD WAR

Permanent installation in Broward Civic Arena, home of NHL Panthers, for 1998

Tactics, strategy, power, force, capture, occupation, victory, defeat, enemy. These words may seem like a description of a war zone, but they also make up the basic vocabulary of many board and field games. Sports such as ice hockey, football, basketball, and soccer and games such as checkers and chess are played on abstracted battlefields – all with a central axis dividing the playing terrain into rival territories. The winner is the first to capture rival pieces or occupy opponent territory. Like institutionalized warfare, sports and games are part of the culture of conquest with highly developed codes of propriety and hostility.

We will appropriate the existing "surface of attraction" – the focal point on which all eyes converge: the ice. Using the 85ft. wide by 200ft. long playing field as a video

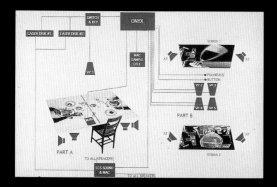

projection screen, we can transform the ice into any fictional surface, at any scale – we can melt it into water, evaporate it into steam, set it on fire, pulverize it to sand. We can utilize a range of illusionistic possibilities and visually stretch the laws of physics. In a series of carefully designed ten-minute computer-assisted videos that exploit the unusual size and orientation of the video image, we intend to foil the expectations of a captive audience perched to witness a sporting event and introduce, instead, a cultural framework of "battle" within which to consider the event to follow.

The project is composed of two major components: the technological system to produce a moving image which fills the ice rink (this includes a computer-controlled matrix of video projectors, suspended above the hockey rink from the equipment grid, and fed by multiple play-back sources), and the video programmes conceived for this system.

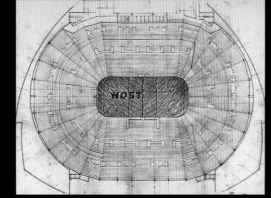

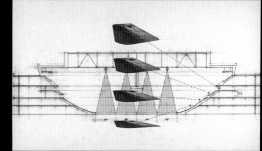

INDIGESTION

Interactive installation in collaboration with the Banff Centre for New Media Research
Script by Douglas Cooper, voices directed by Marianne Weems

Indigestion condenses an archetypal *film noir* narrative into a terse exchange between two characters of ambiguous relation across a dinner table. It is presented in two electronically linked interactive modes: an interactive video and a virtual environment. Systems of *choice* are offered to lure the subject into an interrogation of the democratic aspirations of interactive technologies and to critique reductive binaries such as masculine/ feminine, high class /low class, fact/fiction, and

projected onto a horizontal screen/table that a viewer can join as a guest. There, a touch screen offers character replacements from a variety of gender and class stereotypes. The narrative remains continuous at any switch point though nuanced by differences of character.

In the virtual environment (to be executed at a later date), a participant using a Polhemus motion-sensing device can navigate in real time through the computer-generated, magnified space of the same dinner table. The image is split onto two large screens on opposite sides of the room for 3-D viewing. The mobile, magnified viewpoint across this mega-landscape will reveal a micro-drama played out in detail.

CNN HEADQUARTERS
In collaboration with Romm + Pearsall, Atlanta

Using a combination of information technologies, two media "icons," one in front of the CNN Center and the other inside its atrium, will represent the headquarters of CNN. A "satellite clock" facing Centennial Park combines three synchronized components: a 96 x 30 ft. curved screen of liquid crystal which slowly scrolls a projected earth satellite photo; a video "cab" featuring live broadcasting which climbs up and down the building on an elevator mechanism, timed at half hour intervals according to the Headline

News; and a video marquee at the entrance
cycling through fifteen stations of Turner-
Time/Warner programming.

The interior installation is composed of a
grid of liquid crystal panels suspended across
the atrium. The huge liquid crystal screen
will alternate between large scale video
projections of current news slicing the
atrium space in half, and transparent phases
which retrieve the vast atrium space.

The urban design concept of the UFA Cinema Centre confronts the issue of public space, which is currently endangered in European cities. This situation is caused by the financial insolvency of city governments, which forces the sale of public space to developers, who then propose monofunctional buildings in order to maximize capital return.

By disintegrating the monofunctionality of these structures and adding urban functions to them, a new urbanity can arise in the city. The character of this urbanity would not be determined only by functional differentiation and the creation of new spatial sequences , but also by the injection of media events.

The UFA Cinema Centre is a result of the urban design concept developed for the Pragerstrasse Nord planning competition.

Pragerstrasse was seen as a dynamic spatial sequence, defined by tangents and diagonals rather than by axes.

The interweaving of public squares, public interiors, and passageways was proposed as a way of energizing and densifying the new centre of Dresden.

The junctures between these urban vectors are defined as public spaces.

The UFA Cinema Centre is located at one of these junctures; it is formulated as the urban connection between Pragerplatz and St. Petersburger Strasse. The Cinema itself is thus transformed into a public space.

The Architectural Design Concept
The design is characterized by two intricately interconnected building units: the *Cinema Block*, with eight cinemas and seating for 2600, simultaneously as foyer and public square.

The Cinema Block
The Cinema Block opens up towards the street and is permeable for pedestrian traffic between Pragerstrasse and St. Petersburger Strasse. It is differentiated by the circulation system of the cinemas and by views through to St. Petersburger Strasse.

The Crystal
The Crystal is no longer merely a functional entry hall to the cinemas, but an urban passageway.

The bridges, ramps and stairs to the cinemas are themselves urban expressions. They allow views of the movement of people on a multitude of levels, unfolding the urban space into three dimensions. The lively quality of this space can be described in relation to the dynamic structure of film.

The Skybar, the "floating" double cone inside the foyer, is accessible and will host different functions (café, bar, etc.)

In this way, the content of the building becomes visible to the city as much as the city is visible from the building. It is an inside-out building which sustains a dialogue with the city. The media event, projected from the interior towards the exterior, assists in the creation of urban space.

COOP HIMMELB(L)AU:
Wolf D. Prix
Helmut Swiczinsky+Partner
Project Leader: Tom Wiscombe
Project Team: Sally Bibawy,
Rainer Enk, Waltraud Hoheneder,
Walid Janj, Nerma Liensberger,
Verena Perius, Florian Pfeifer,
James Puckhaber,
Andreas Schaller,
Karolin Schmidbaur,
Alexander Seitlinger,
Bernd Spiess,
Andreas Westhausser,
Andreas Wohofsky, Susanne Zottl.

Structural Engineering:
Bollinger+Grohmann/Frankfurt

Under construction.
Completion date: early 1998.

Site/context model
OPPOSITE: Crystal detail model

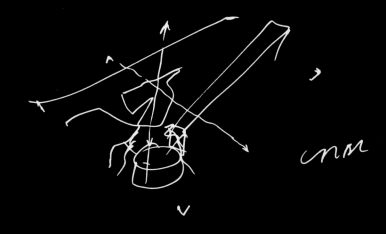

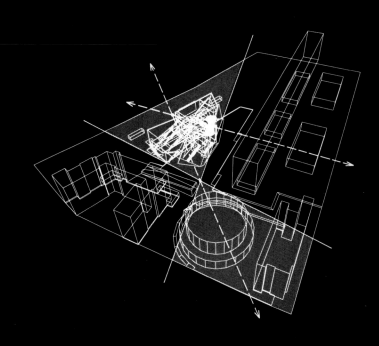

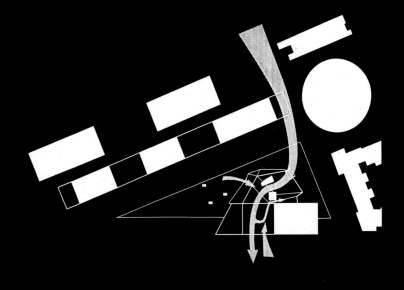

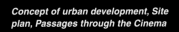

Concept of urban development, Site plan, Passages through the Cinema

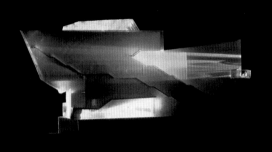

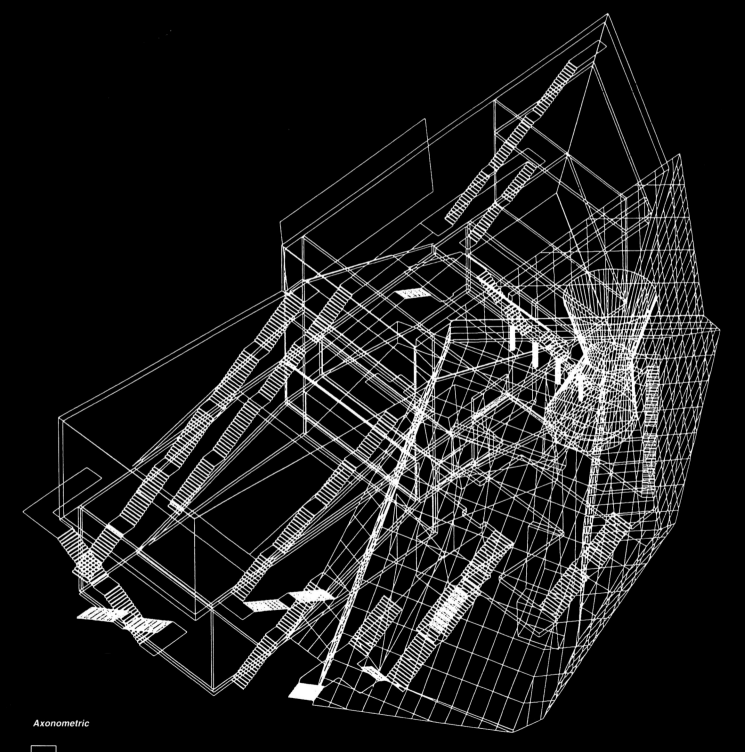

Axonometric

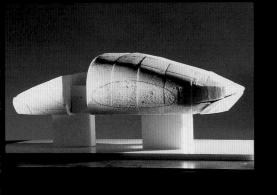

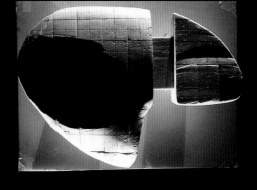

Models of the Foyer, not built

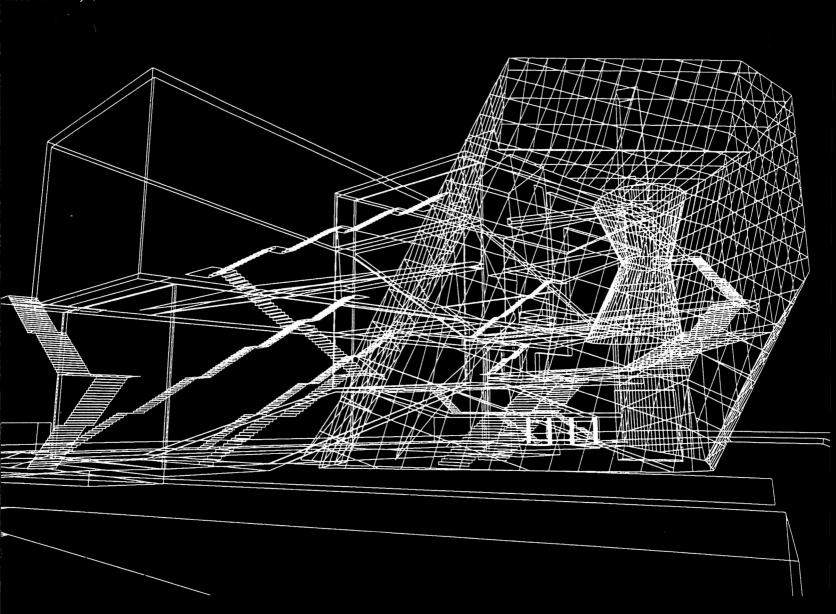

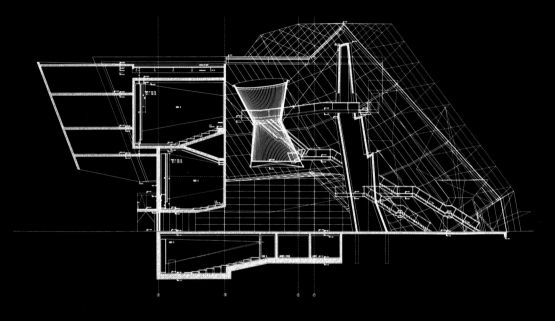

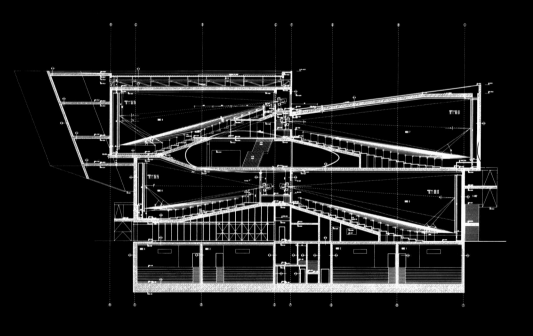

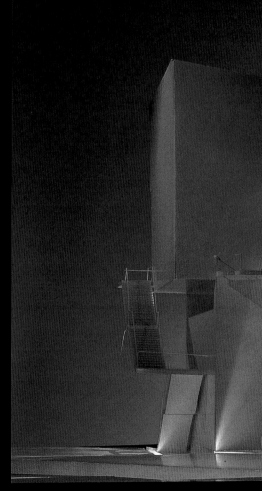

Sections

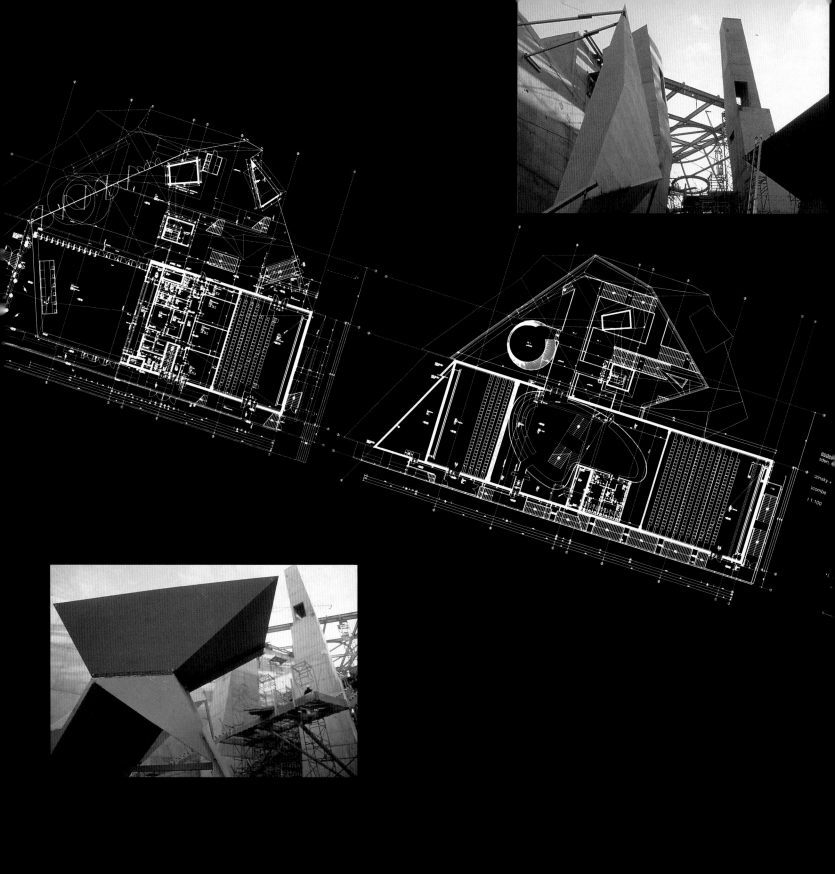

esde
sden,
zinsky +
scombe
1:100

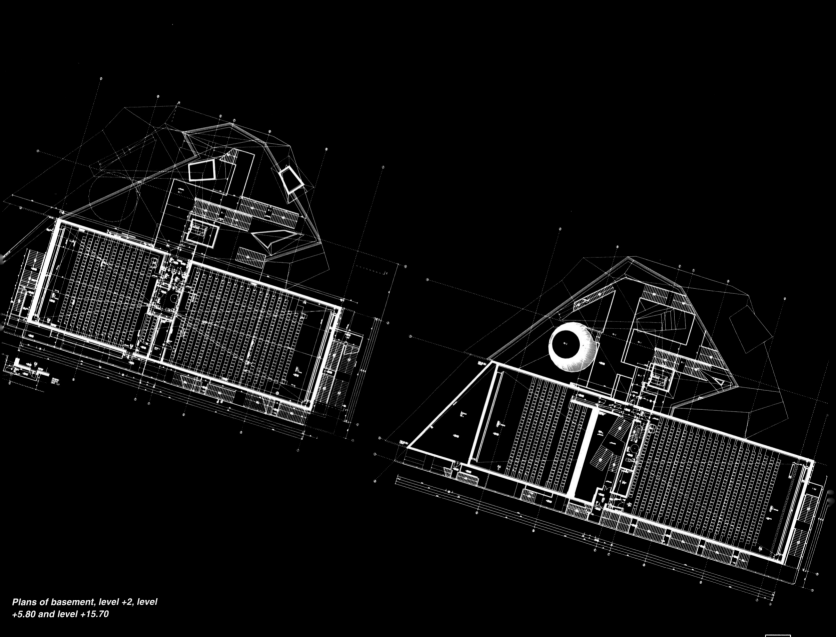

Plans of basement, level +2, level
+5.80 and level +15.70

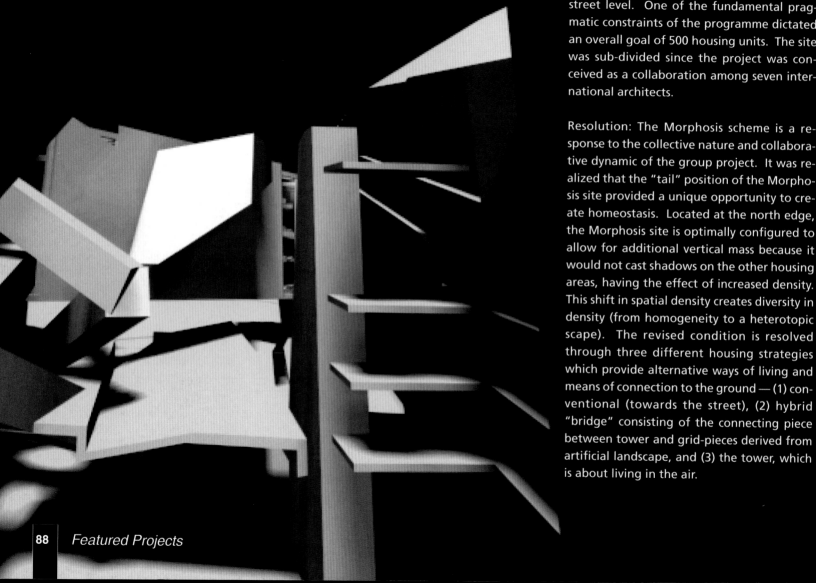

street level. One of the fundamental prag-
matic constraints of the programme dictated
an overall goal of 500 housing units. The site
was sub-divided since the project was conceived as a collaboration among seven international architects.

Resolution: The Morphosis scheme is a response to the collective nature and collaborative dynamic of the group project. It was realized that the "tail" position of the Morphosis site provided a unique opportunity to create homeostasis. Located at the north edge,
the Morphosis site is optimally configured to
allow for additional vertical mass because it
would not cast shadows on the other housing
areas, having the effect of increased density.
This shift in spatial density creates diversity in
density (from homogeneity to a heterotopic
scape). The revised condition is resolved
through three different housing strategies
which provide alternative ways of living and
means of connection to the ground — (1) conventional (towards the street), (2) hybrid
"bridge" consisting of the connecting piece
between tower and grid-pieces derived from
artificial landscape, and (3) the tower, which
is about living in the air.

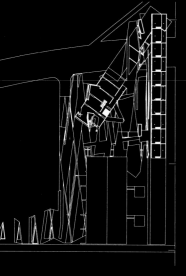

Morphosis

Wagrammerstrasse, Vienna Housing, and Sun Tower, Seoul

The ground level plane of artificial landscape is the departure point of Morphosis's geometric spatial strategy. An artificial "landscape" is a mimetic device that describes the interstitial "sub-urban" condition. The artificial landscape is folded and cut so that the interwoven horizontal planes are in flux. The main pedestrian entrance into the court is through a "bridge" that is a presence in a void created by cut-outs. These cut-outs allow natural light to penetrate into the subterranean parking structure. As well as enhancing the spatial and light quality of subterranean spaces, the lattice of the artificial landscape frames civic open spaces for community functions and is also a transitional element to the adjacent scheme. Vertical movement via tower elevators is accessed through this court.

The entire scheme is connected underground with a vehicular entrance accessed via Eipeldauerstraße. A subterranean street parallel to Wagrammerstraße services the retail spaces and provides access to the parking spaces. The parking areas are organized in a helix configuration of shifting planes. These produce alternating levels of natural light, and thus are idiosyncratic, identifiable and individualized spaces.

Date of Design: 1995

SUN TOWER, SEOUL

Site: The site is 400 sq.m. in Seoul, Korea. The context is a district of two-storey commercial buildings with a concentration of pedestrian traffic adjacent to EWHA, Korea's largest women's university.

Programme: Our client, a sportswear manufacturer, requested a high-profile building to create a youthful and sophisticated image as the base for their international enterprise. The interiors specified retail accoutrements on five floors (including two basements) and offices for their international corporate headquarters in the penthouse.

Resolution: The architecture wraps around a central wedge-shaped volume of space that functions as an exterior court. To maximize visual activity, vertical circulation fronts the exterior walls that face the court. The building is clad in perforated steel that is conceptually linked to clothing and fabric, but at an urban scale. The perforated steel is attached as panels with lights positioned behind it, creating a billboard-scale sign. The electrified surface creates a nocturnal transformation, thus a dual character between day and night.

Date of Completion: Spring 1996

WAGRAMMERSTRASSE, VIENNA HOUSING
Client: Herbert Binder, City of Vienna
Coordinator: Markus Spiegelfeld
Principal: Thom Mayne
Project Architect: Kim Groves
Project Designer: Kristina Loock
Project Team: Dave Grant
Project Assistants: Erik Anderson
Laith Al-Sayigh
Mark Briggs
Gavin Hutcheson
Richard Koschitz
Jelena Mijanovic
Ludovica Milo
Chris Peck

SUN TOWER, SEOUL
Clients: Jae Kwon Kim
Steven Kim
Principal: Thom Mayne
Project Designers: Dave Grant
Kristina Loock
Eui-Sung Yi
Kim Groves
Project Manager: Eul-ho Suh
Project Assistants: Jay Behr
Mark Briggs
Neil Crawford
Towan Kim
Janice Shimizu
Richard Koschitz
Joint Venture Architect / Engineers: Daisung
Project Architect: Kwan Kim Soo

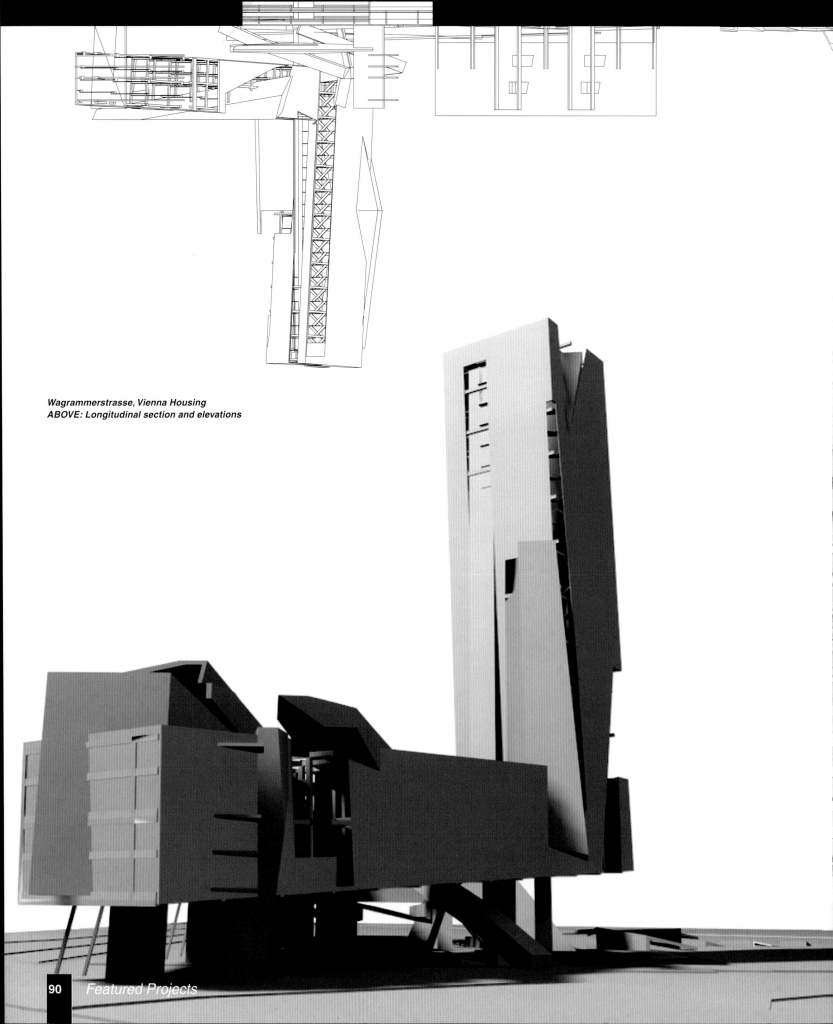

Wagrammerstrasse, Vienna Housing
ABOVE: Longitudinal section and elevations

Sun Tower, Seoul

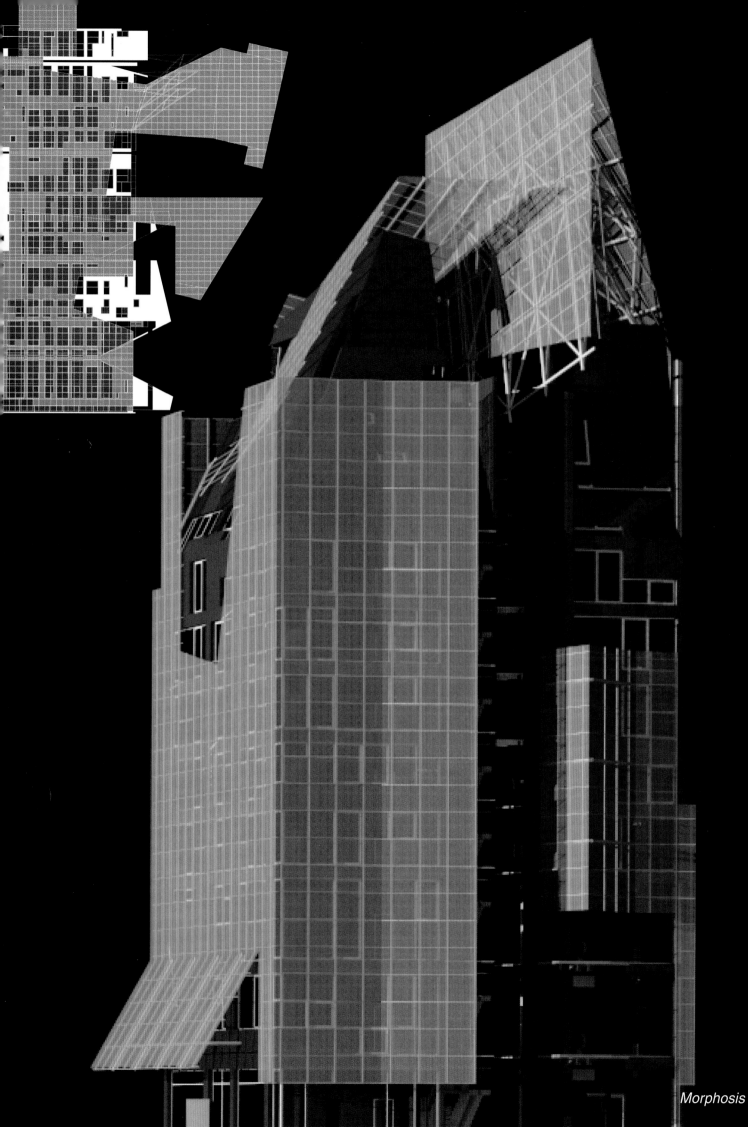

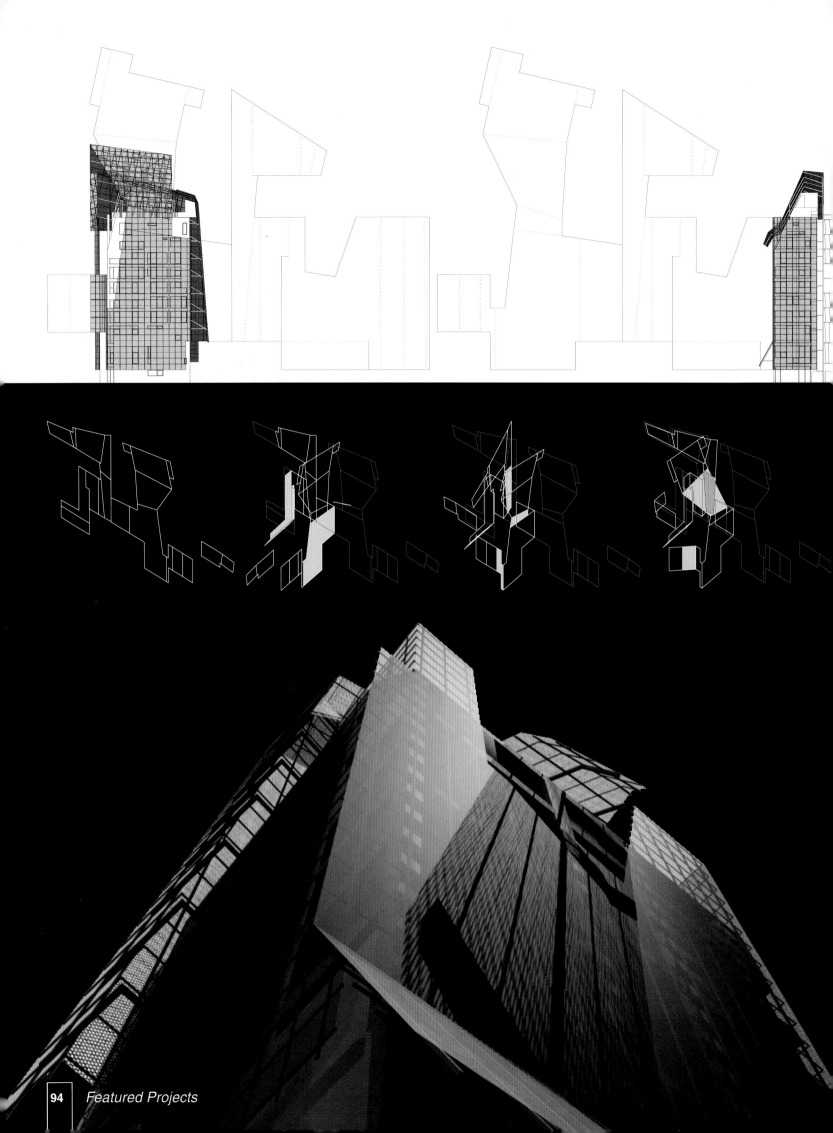

Sun Tower, Seoul
ABOVE: West elevation, North elevation,
East elevation, Skin and Screen
LEFT: Axonometrics

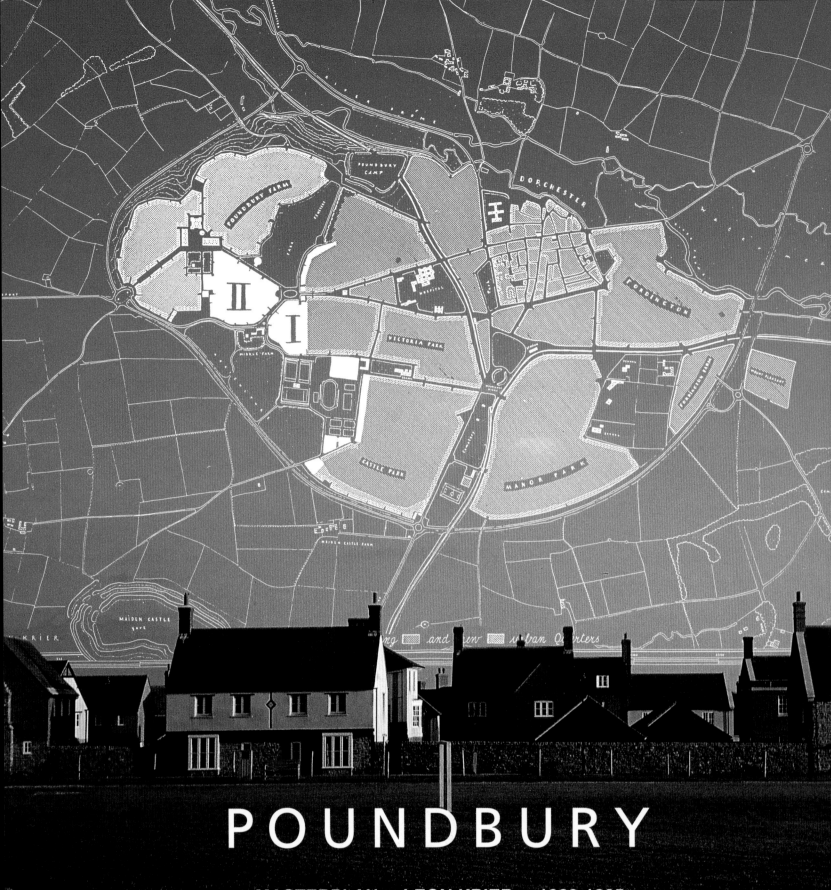

POUNDBURY

MASTERPLAN   LEON KRIER   1989-1995

ABOVE; PHASE I AND PHASE II CURRENTLY UNDER CONSTRUCTION
BELOW: POUNDBURY – MIDDLE FARM QUARTER – TOWN EDGE FROM WEST

Architects: Graham Saunders, Peter John Smyth, Ken Morgan

After years of wholesale condemnation by the media *The Independent*'s recent headline "AND THE PRINCE HAS GOT IT RIGHT" announces a sea change in the reporting on Poundbury. With the Duchy of Cornwall's Dorset development, the Prince of Wales's vision is becoming a built, lived in, worked in, truly modern reality; people like it and they buy into it; the clientele is as varied as the architecture; there is no social, functional, or architectural uniformity. Poundbury is not a philanthropic experiment; it is not an endowed development; it works on the basis of the logic of the market, by supply and demand. It does not have the status of a new town; it has no state funding to pay for its infrastructure. It is not a unique experiment but is eminently reproducible. Despite its blacklisting by the modernist culture mafia, word is spreading, both nationally and internationally, that Poundbury is a model for desirable development.

In December 1997 building started on the last section of Phase I: the Middle Farm quarter. Ninety-seven per cent of the buildings have been sold off the drawing board, an unusual occurrence in the United Kingdom and proof of the extraordinary market success of a radically "different" experiment.

At the same time the first urban industrial complex of Phase II is nearing completion and another 40,000 sq.ft. industry is laying foundations. While modernist critics continue to pour scorn on their preferred target, some of

the first settlers are reselling their homes at a profit in order to acquire larger properties in the new Middle Farm section. There are more than 270 applicants for the 40 units in the Renaissance Centre, condemned by the local press as "Kolditz Krier." Disproving the predictions of established real estate experts, there now exists a waiting list for non-residential uses (industrial, commercial, offices) exceeding all expectations. All of which proves that the free market is (a) not conservative when given a choice; (b) not anti-social, anti-aesthetic or anti-urban when given a chance.

Poundbury has literally been developed without a development programme. There is no preconceived programme of buildings and uses. The masterplan consists essentially of a building-plot plan and a set of development principles. The attitude towards uses avoids uniformity and area zoning and is inclusive rather than exclusive. It is essentially open to any market demand, which is directed towards an adequate plot – the largest being 80,000 sq.ft., the smallest 1,500 sq.ft. Large plots are always located on the edge of each quarter where they are easily reached by heavy vehicles. The most prominent sites and plots are reserved for public buildings and uses. These do not have any preconceived programme either. When the need arises for a squash club, a school, a cemetery, or a village hall, plots that satisfy the client as well as the masterplanner are available.

Photography: Léon Krier
Masterplan: Léon Krier
Development Director: Andrew Hamilton
West Dorset District Architect: David Oliver
Coordinating architect: Peterjohn Smyth (Percy Thomas Partnership)
Planner and Infrastructural Engineer: Alan Baxter Associates
Architects for Phase I individual buildings: Trevor Harris, Clive Hawkins, Ken Morgan, David Oliver, Graham Saunders, Sidell Gibson Partnership, Peterjohn Smyth, Liam O'Connor, John Souter, Robert Taylor

Architect: Graham Saunders

Traffic and the Geometry of Public Spaces
All streets, avenues, mews, even passages and alleys are designed to be good spaces, i.e., they are not mere leftovers; they do not run carelessly from horizon to horizon; they do not run idiotically into dead ends. Some focus on buildings, others on the landscape. Within the quarters, streets are relatively short and winding. Meanders that slow down rivers do the same to traffic flows, without the use of signs or gadgets. Only the Parkway and the avenues dividing the quarters and focusing on major landscape or built features run relatively or even dead straight. This extremely varied geometric pattern not only establishes an unusually wide hierarchical scale of road types, but it encourages varied and subtle behaviour from drivers, inducing more urbane, less mechanical reactions.

ARCHITECTS: TREVOR HARRIS - CLIVE HAWKINS - KEN MORGAN

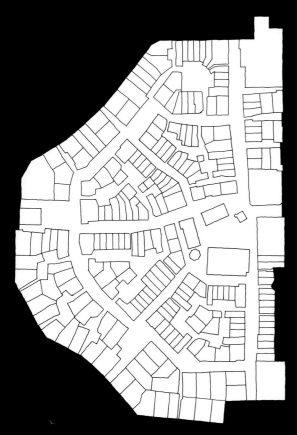

BUILDING PLOTS, PHASE I

The free geometry of Poundbury's public spaces marries naturally with the simplicity and practicality of vernacular architecture. The clear individuality of each building does not contradict the harmony of the whole. The production costs of standard modern houses and factories, while permitting an authentic vernacular are not able to realize grand architectural effects; this is one of the many reasons why in Poundbury monumental architecture is reserved for major public buildings.

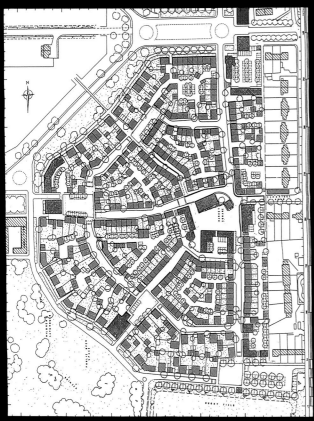

PHASE I, MIDDLE FARM QUARTER

SIDELL GIBSON PARTNERSHIP - GRAHAM SAUNDERS - KEN MORGAN

GRAHAM SAUNDERS - KEN MORGAN

SIDELL GIBSON PARTNERSHIP

CLIVE HAWKINS · GRAHAM SAUNDERS · PETER JOHN SMYTH · CLIVE HAWKINS · KEN MORGAN   TYPICAL BLOCK WITH PARKING MEWS

KEN MORGAN - CLIVE HAWKINS - PETERJOHN SMYTH - GRAHAM SAUNDERS - CLIVE HAWKINS

PETERJOHN SMYTH - GRAHAM SAUNDERS - CLIVE HAWKINS

GRAHAM SAUNDERS

Leon Krier 101

POUNDBURY PHASE II, MASTERPLAN BY LEON KRIER 1995

The guiding principle of functional distribution is to achieve in each completed urban quarter a checkerboard dispersal of uses, i.e. a mix of large and small neighbouring plots, of residential and non-residential, of private and institutional uses. Some blocks consist of a single plot, others of several plots, but they always form coherent urban frontages onto a street, an avenue, a square or an alley. Private space is clearly separated from public space by buildings and high masonry walls. Industrial production hangars, office premises and artisan

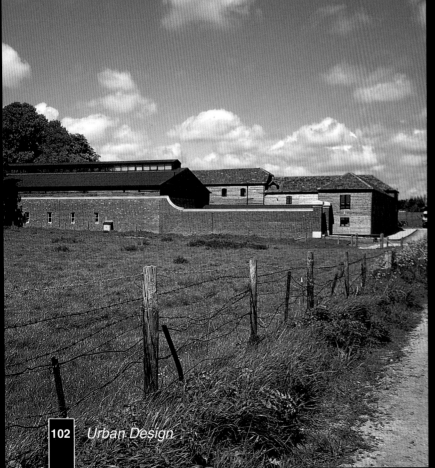

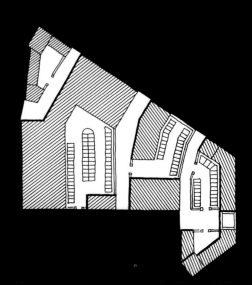

BUILDING PLOTS, PHASE II

workshops are grouped around private parking courtyards. In combination with the typical parking mews this concept achieves a very high parking capacity (one car per 25 sq.m. of floor space) with a low visual impact on the townscape.

The variety of block and plot configurations and sizes, each occupied by a different use, forms the basis for true architectural variety. Each building looks different from its neighbours for existential rather than styling reasons.

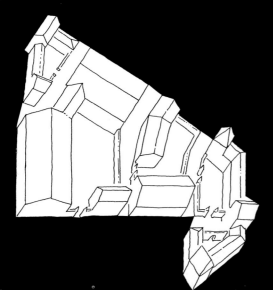

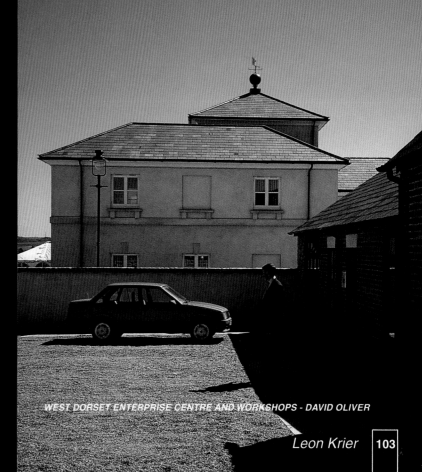

WEST DORSET ENTERPRISE CENTRE AND WORKSHOPS - DAVID OLIVER

The success of the realization of Poundbury's masterplan is due largely to a rudimentary command structure and the open human relationships within that structure, all subordinated to the same architectural and urban vision. Even a brilliant, sophisticated masterplan leads to poor results if openness is missing in the everyday management of such an instrument. Poundbury's Middle Farm Quarter and Hardye School are both guided by the same masterplan and philosophy but with divergeant and discordant results. The designers and buildings of Poundbury followed the vision with ardour and conviction; those of Hardye School paid mere lipservice to the idea. It is these differing responses that ensure authenticity on the one hand but result in kitsch simulacra on the other.

Graham Saunders - Sidell Gibson Partnership - Ken Morgan - Graham Saunders

Graham Saunders - Clive Hawkins

Middle Farm buildings are designed by individual architects, working for individual clients and small builders. This conscious choice made Poundbury's "difference" possible; the Duchy of Cornwall could have chosen an easier path by selling the whole site to bulk buildiers with predictable results. The Prince of Wales knew from experience that the margins of such organizations do not allow them to experiment with new forms of development. The moderate to small development phases and building plots allow small builders and developers to be competitive. They have lower running costs and a better knowledge of local building materials and the local labour market. Craft-based artisans and builders are a pre-condition to producing an authentic, i.e. a tectonically and stylistically correct architectural vernacular.

Leon Krier is the author of Architecture: Choice or Fate, *recently published by Papadakis, Windsor*

Graham Saunders - Ken Morgan - Sidell Gibson Partnership - Graham Saunders

Poundbury Bench. Design by Léon Krier. Produced by Stephen Florence

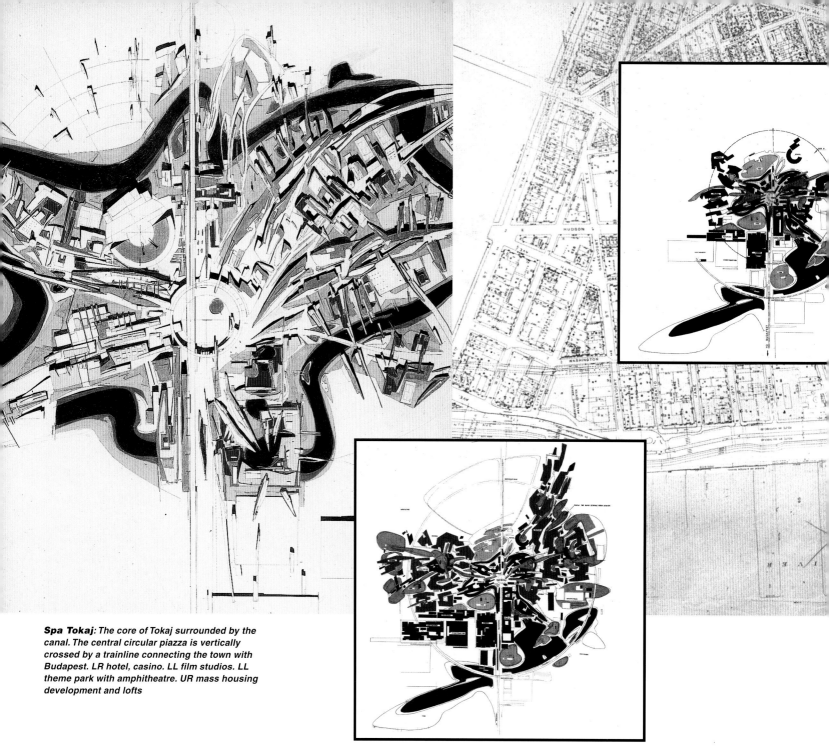

Spa Tokaj: *The core of Tokaj surrounded by the canal. The central circular piazza is vertically crossed by a trainline connecting the town with Budapest. LR hotel, casino. LL film studios. LL theme park with amphitheatre. UR mass housing development and lofts*

Spa Tokaj, Phase 2: *Further development. Dark grey: existing built structures. Grey: proposed housing development north-west and east of city centre. Light grey: network of parks organized into greenways connects city centre with nature*

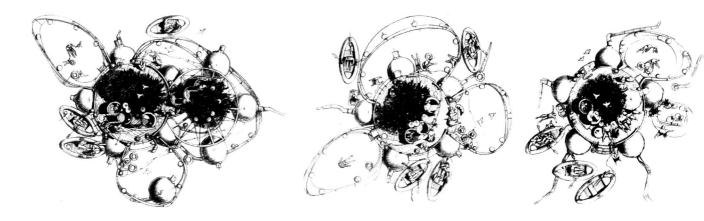

The Michael Sorkin Studio

Michael Sorkin + Andrei Vovk

Spa Tokaj, Phase 1: *Initial development. Black: lake and canal surrounding the town core. Dark grey: proposed building development. Light grey: initiation of penetrating network of parks and inner green space to connect the town centre with surrounding nature.*

OUT OF CONTROL

Cities are organic. These projects are about the growth and decay of the city, about a phenomenon that resists discipline, and about the effort to impose just the right amount. Good planning is coercive: like farming or gardening, it tries to provoke a particular effect. The politics of planning lies in building and recognizing the right fantasies of desirability from which to proceed. The urban contract is always a moment of agreement between freedom and constraint, the regulating framework for private expression.

Each of these projects grows from the culture and architecture on its site. There is nothing ex nihilo here: for widespread growth, many seeds are required. Only such multiplicity can produce a system that promises — to our great delight — to grow out of our control.

Westside Waterfront: *Public transportation network. Blue lines: proposed waterways around Manhattan Island. Red lines: proposed ground transportation. Red circles: transfer stops along the Hudson river waterfront. Yellow: waterfront neighbourhoods affected by the scheme.*

Spa Tokaj, Hungary, 1995

A project for a small town with industries of pleasure and health near Budapest began with an entrepreneur's speculation about a recreational development leveraged on the construction of new facilities for the recently privatized Hungarian film industry. Tokaj expands this programme to the proportions of a town, adding housing, commerce, schools, cultural facilities and other infrastructure. It also adds spa and casino to the mix.

The centre of town — bounded by a sinewy canal — is free of all cars and linked to Budapest by rail. Vehicular traffic circulates on a perimeter road that feeds parking lots and service tunnels. Delineated to foot-ranges, surrounded by parks, lakes, athletic facilities, and agriculture, Tokaj would expand in two phases to a radius of approximately 1500m. At build-out, the town would include two additional neighbourhood centres in addition to the activities fronting the main plaza. Greenery penetrates in strong vectors to the centre of town, allowing unimpeded walks from backyard to open countryside.

Michael Sorkin - principal
Andrei Vovk - partner
Yukiko Yokoo - associate
Mitchell Joachim
Victoria Marshall

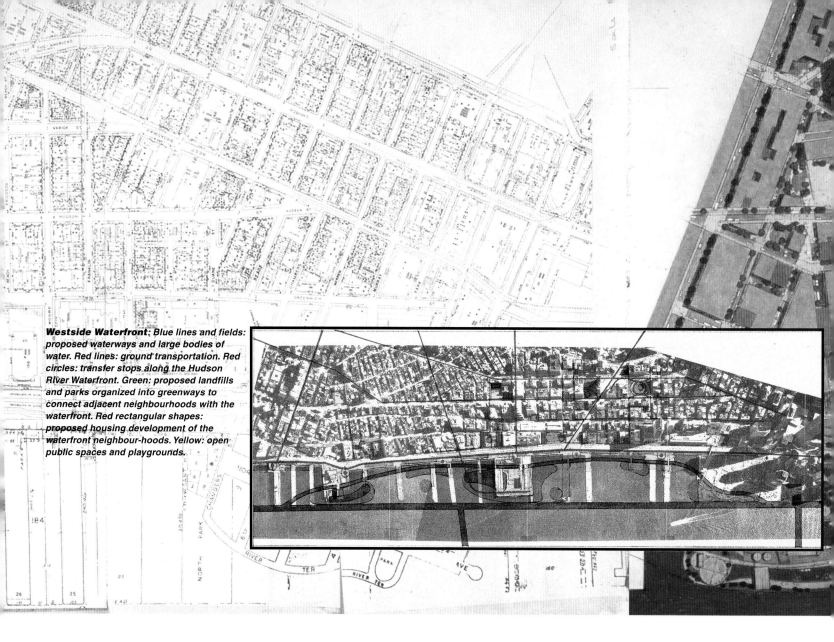

Westside Waterfront: *Blue lines and fields: proposed waterways and large bodies of water. Red lines: ground transportation. Red circles: transfer stops along the Hudson River Waterfront. Green: proposed landfills and parks organized into greenways to connect adjacent neighbourhoods with the waterfront. Red rectangular shapes: proposed housing development of the waterfront neighbour-hoods. Yellow: open public spaces and playgrounds.*

Westside Waterfront, New York City, 1995-97

In this unsolicited plan for the Hudson river waterfront from Fourteenth Street to Battery Park City the site was studied both as a place and a condition. For years, the water's edge has been in almost constant and often rapid motion, carved and filled by the construction, enlargement and decay of piers, by shifts in use, and by the comings and goings of ships and boats. This dynamic, amphibious, waterfront not only extends outwards to the pier line but inland to the streets and avenues. Sixth Avenue has been taken as the "shore-line" for this particular study.

The waterfront interacts with the city both across and along the water's edge.

Waterborne transportation is crucial. To make it possible, it is important that boats be able to sail and dock at the bulkhead line. A channel is proposed at land's edge for water buses and taxis to ease the transfer from boats to other forms of motion. This channel also solves the problem of the squared off Battery Park landfill which — by interrupting the ebb and the flow of the river — has created a biological dead zone at its north end.

New waterside uses in the plan are entirely recreational or community, and include parks, marinas, restaurants, bath-house, beaches, boatyards, etc. While the opportunities for making new parks at large scale in lower Man-

hattan are largely confined to the waterfront, it is, however, also possible to create a system of smaller scale parks on vacant lots, traffic islands, and other left-over spaces, a "parkapelago" of green islets.

A policy of "Greenfill" is also proposed. The select removal of parking lanes on downtown streets would immediately slow traffic. The new space — raised to sidewalk level — is used for consolidating waste and recycling. The number of street trees is increased by 100%. Bicycle storage is provided. Community gardening sheds are erected. Benches, playspaces, and gardens, even small child-care centres or community huts appear.

Floating Islands, Hamburg, 1997

A public art proposal commissioned by the city of Hamburg for the Binnen Alster, a lake-sized body of water in the middle of the city, these floating green islands are meant to move lazily in the wind and currents, sometimes lashed together to form larger surfaces for use. Breaking away, they drift around the lake, stopping now and then to join other activities. A number of these islands are to be 'living machines,' bio-remediation devices capable of cleaning the surrounding water to swimming quality. Others offer sunbathing on deck chairs and recliners, picnicking on the grass. Table tennis islands, whose surfaces are never quite still, challenge your game.

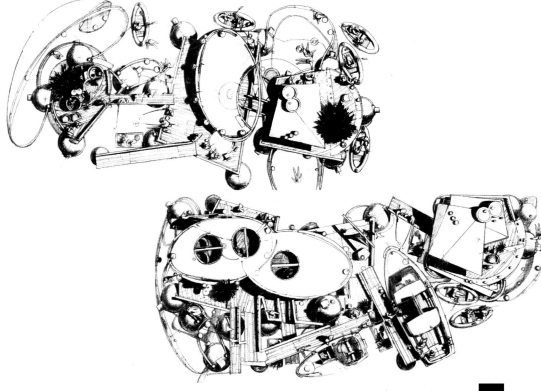

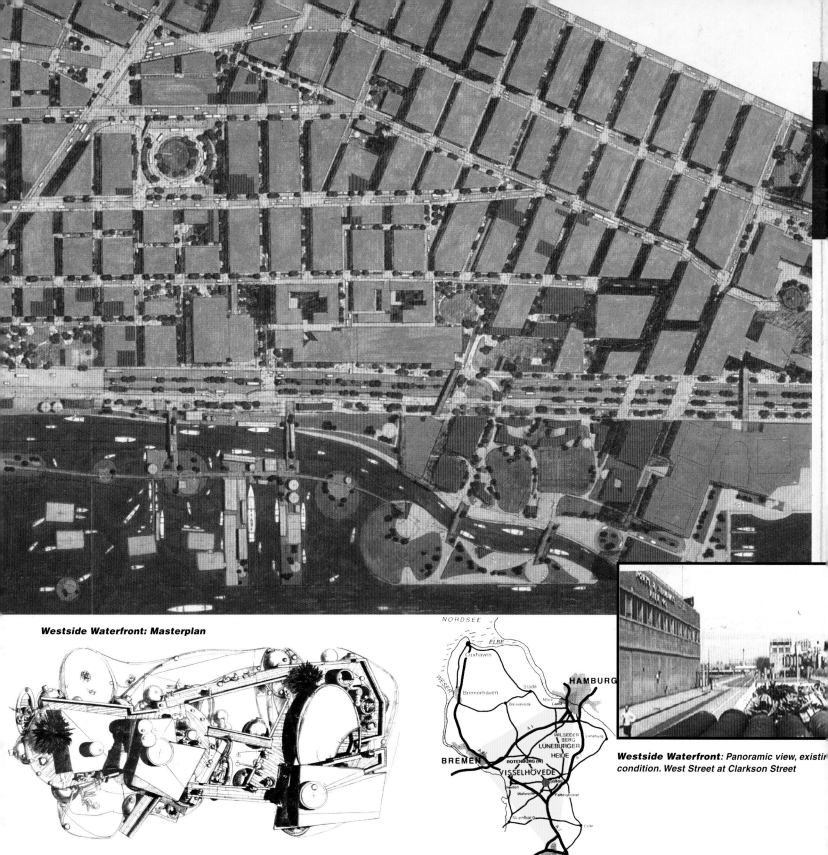

Westside Waterfront: Masterplan

Westside Waterfront: *Panoramic view, existing condition. West Street at Clarkson Street*

Visselhoevede, Germany, 1996

Michael Sorkin was approached by an environmental research institute to work with a small town in northern Germany which faced a dramatic decline in agricultural production owing to a very unfavourable competitive position within the European Union. The Institute had persuaded the town that there was a bright future in the technologies of the information age. The town officials themselves wanted to increase the population by approximately 2,500 in addition to the current popu-

lation of 13,000, sustain a high school and maintain the level of services desired by the citizens.

The proposed plan freezes the growth of existing settlements and builds new ribbon developments surrounding a series of new "green living rooms" – agricultural lobes consolidated in the most fertile areas. Farming becomes the daily foreground of the ribbon-dwellers. Land formerly under cultivation would become a park, the town lung, play-

ground and industry.

A series of small new ribbon-centres would contain basic neighbourhood apparatus, including corner shops, child-care and other services, and a small amount of loft-space devoted to collective use by people who – while liking to "telecommute" – still prefer to work in the company of others.

A new circulation infrastructure has been designed for non-automotive traffic that will include walkers, bikers, horseback-riders, as well as small slo-mo electrics.

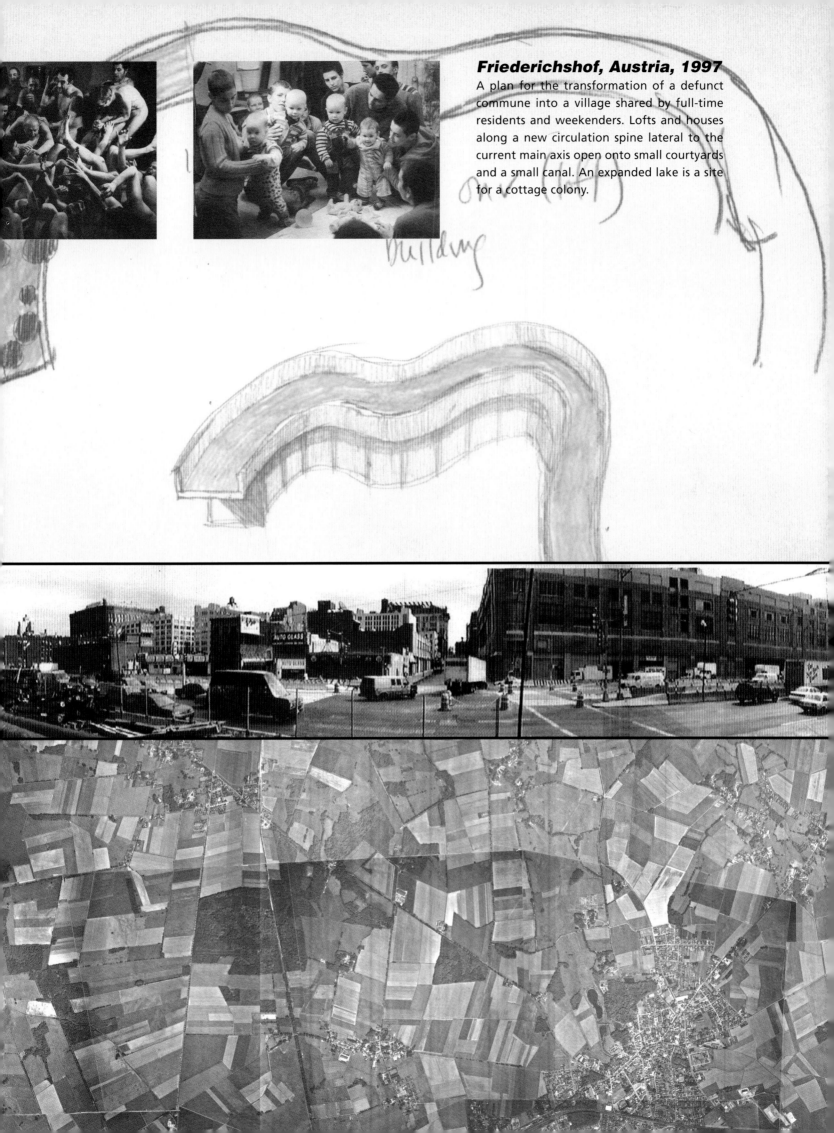

Friederichshof, Austria, 1997
A plan for the transformation of a defunct commune into a village shared by full-time residents and weekenders. Lofts and houses along a new circulation spine lateral to the current main axis open onto small courtyards and a small canal. An expanded lake is a site for a cottage colony.

Westside Waterfront: *Pink: proposed new buildings and roof-top additions to existing buildings. Yellow: wide pedestrian crossings*

Friederichshof, Austria, Phase 1: Red: existing buildings. Pink: proposed buildings. Grey: roads and parking. Blue: existing lake. Yellow: paths and playing fields. Green: open space.

Phase 2: Pink: building development, continuation of Phase 1. Blue: new lake, canal, and courtyard ponds.

Visselhoevede: Phase 1. Yellow fields: agricultural 'lobes.' Pink rectangles: housing to be developed along sides of the 'lobes.' Blue lines: public ground transportation, 'call-a-bus.' Red circles: bus stops; housing development starts within 500m of each bus stop.

Visselhoevede: Yellow fields

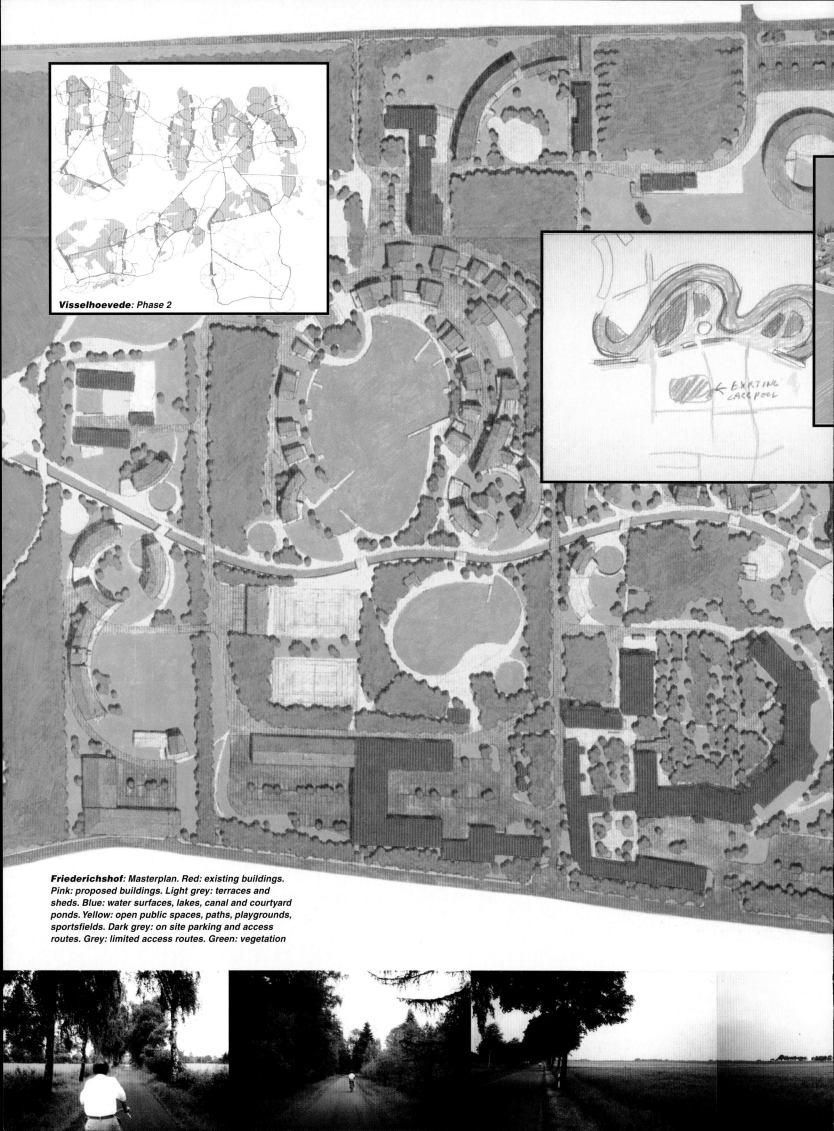

Visselhoevede: *Phase 2*

←EXISTING CESSPOOL

Friederichshof: *Masterplan. Red: existing buildings. Pink: proposed buildings. Light grey: terraces and sheds. Blue: water surfaces, lakes, canal and courtyard ponds. Yellow: open public spaces, paths, playgrounds, sportsfields. Dark grey: on site parking and access routes. Grey: limited access routes. Green: vegetation*

Friederichshof: Aerial view today

Friederichshof: Aerial view. Proposed two- to four-storey buildings in a landscaped park.

Jack Ox - From Merz to Ur
Kurt Schwitters Hanover *Merzbau* and *Ursonate*
Visual reinterpretation and realization

KURT SCHWITTERS' HANOVER MERZBAU AND URSONATE by Gisela Hossmann

Full of dadaistic wit and irony, Kurt Schwitters once noted "Ewig währt am Längsten" ("Eternity lasts longest"). This remark gave him and the extraordinary oeuvre he left behind some kind of absolute immortality.

Born in 1887 in Hanover, he died in 1948 in his English exile in Ambleside in the Lake District where he spent the last years of his life as a refugee from Nazi Germany.

During the 1920s and 1930s Schwitters created two of his most characteristic and important works: the *Merzbau* and the *Ursonate*. One is a bizarre architectural installation, the other an abstract phonetic poem composed like a piece of music.

The Merzbau. The beginning of what was later known as *Merzbau* was several isolated dadaistic sculptures. When the space between these sculptures became too narrow, the artist combined them into one and thus a new work was born, the so-called Säule (Column).

At the same time the artist created a large number of Merz-paintings, Merz-collages of everyday materials and objects found in the streets, as well as spacious reliefs with grottoes and hollows. When there was no more space in the studio, all these different parts merged into one single artefact which outgrew the studio walls, spread into adjacent rooms and finally took possession of the artist's house. Thus, from 1919 until 1937 a total art work was built from constructive and organic elements which Kurt Schwitters had to leave behind unfinished and unguarded when he emigrated to Norway before World War II. The *Merzbau*, which the artist first called *Kathedrale des erotische Elenda* (Cathedral of Erotic Misery) was the first art installation of the twentieth century. Its influence and impact on all following generations of artists was tremendous — and still is today.

In 1943 when the house and studio of Kurt Schwitters in Hanover were destroyed by bombs, his unique masterpiece also disappeared. In his Norwegian exile the artist began a new *Merzbau*, but this was destroyed by fire in 1951; and his third attempt to realize such a total art work in his English home was still unfinished when he died in 1948.

His first *Merzbau*, which he developed as a work in progress over more than fifteen years, became the authentic icon of dadaistic art. A part reconstruction is on display at the Sprangel Museum in Schwitters' home town of Hanover.

The Ursonate. Coming back from a trip to Prague in 1921, Kurt Schwitters began work on another extraordinary dadaistic oeuvre: the *Ursonate*. Fascinated by the phonetic poem of his friend Raoul Hausmann *fmsbw*, Schwitters started to compose his own phonetic poem like a piece of music with four movements and different individual themes.

Like all of his Merz paintings, his *Merzbau* and all the other works of the 1920s and 1930s, this subtly constructed poem is based on the collage technique which he mastered so brilliantly. While for his paintings, reliefs and sculptures he used all kinds of ordinary materials and objects, the poem is based only on the phonetic elements of language. These elements are organized according to the principles of composition. The poem consists not only of isolated and senseless sounds, but of individual words such as *rakete* or *PRA* (the inversion of the name of his friend Arp).

In 1932 the complete *Ursonate* was first published in Schwitters' magazine *Merz 24* as a concrete poem constructed by Jan Tachichold, a Swiss typographer. Kurt Schwitters himself recited his poetic work several times in public and, in 1925, the first record was published with parts of the *Ursonate* spoken by the author himself. Another recording, which was taken in 1932 and had long been lost, was rediscovered recently by the American artist Jack Ox during her research work on Schwitters' *Ursonate* for her visual translation of this poem. Now this unique recording is available on compact disc.

Like the *Merzbau*, which was of enormous influence on the post-war generations of visual artists, the *Ursonate* deeply influenced the concrete poetry of this period. Even today, avant-garde art and literature would be unimaginable without the ideas and work of Kurt Schwitters.   *Gisela Hossmann*

VISUAL REINTERPRETATION AND REALIZATION BY JACK OX

Almost fifty years after Kurt Schwitters' death, his ideas are the source of much that is "cutting edge" in the 1990s. Schwitters' *Merzbau* was the first living, organically growing installation; his *Ursonate* is the precursor of Intermedia art which flourishes today; and the collage, an art form which he developed from the invention of Picasso and Braque, has become the language of choice in all contemporary art forms.

In 1991 the American Intermedia artist Jack Ox, while living in Cologne, Germany, began her 800 sq.ft. visualization of the *Ursonate*.

Ox has been making visual "translations" or re-orchestrations of extant musical compositions since the 1970s. Her accumulated opus includes Gregorian Chant, J.S. Bach, I. Stravinsky, C. Debussy, and all the themes from A. Bruckner's eighth symphony, shown in 1996 in Austria.

Ox's self-created language has visual equivalents for melody, time, rhythm, harmonic movement and qualities, and depends upon traditional musicological analysis. The *Ursonate*, being a single voiced sound poem, albeit written in a nineteenth-century sonata form, also necessitated the use of phonetics as an analytical device. There is a system of transparent colours, painted over the thematic images, which represents the various vowel sounds. Consonants are produced through specific collage patterns of the syllables.

Jack Ox's *Ursonate* uses images from Kurt Schwitters' various *Merzbau* constructions and landscapes from his World War II exile in Norway and England's Lake District. She chose the Hanover *Merzbau* to represent the largest and most important theme: Fümms bö wö tää zää Uu, pögiff, Kwii Ee. Ox used archive *Merzbau* photographs, the only existing record of this destroyed masterpiece, to make her drawing and print of the original Schwitters' installation. She turned the irregularly shaped elements in her mind, melding the three photographs into a single perspectival system. Each syllable of the theme was assigned a specific part of the drawing. These would appear in four different scale possibilities, depending on how loudly they were spoken by Schwitters in his own recording. His melody can be seen through a shifting up and down of the image fragments. All silences in the original composition are represented by very bright solid colours, beginning with a deep red for the longest pause, and ending with a green-yellow for a short breath.

In effect, Jack Ox has subjected Kurt Schwitters' three dimensional Constructivist collage to a further very formal, algorithmic collage process, which takes its cue from Information Theory. It is a marriage, or interweaving, of two distinctly different eras in the twentieth century.

Jack Ox's *Ursonate* installation was recently exhibited at the Podewil in **Berlin**, Germany, together with a performance by Dary John Mizelle. It will be exhibited at the Alstervilla Foundation for the Support of Contemporary Art in **Hamburg**, Germany, in April.

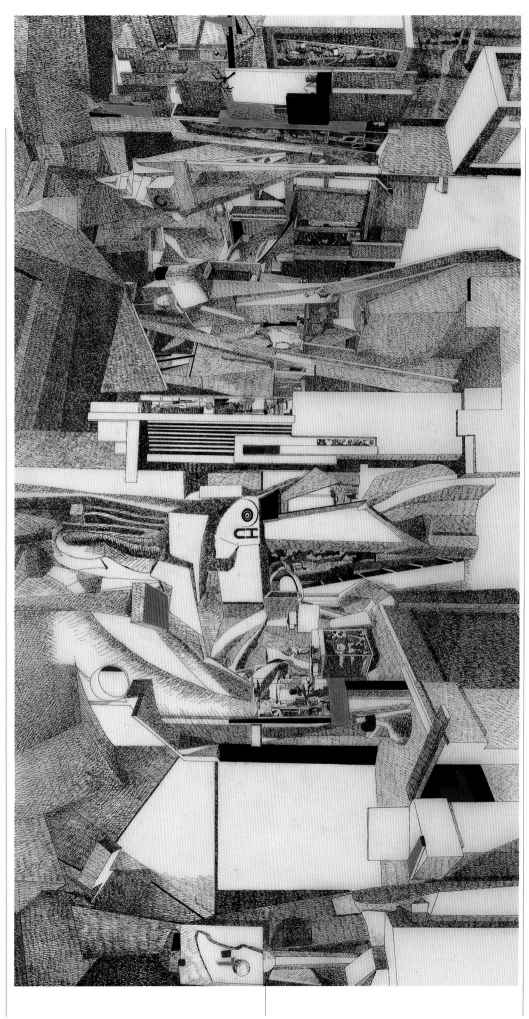

Kurt Schwitters' Hanover **Merzbau** *which was drawn by Jack Ox and used as the first visual theme of her visualization of the* Ursonate. *This theme is* Fümms bö wö tää zää Uu, pögiff, Kwii Ee. *Electrostatic transfer on mylar, hand coloured with colour pencil, 88 x 160cm.*

Jack Ox

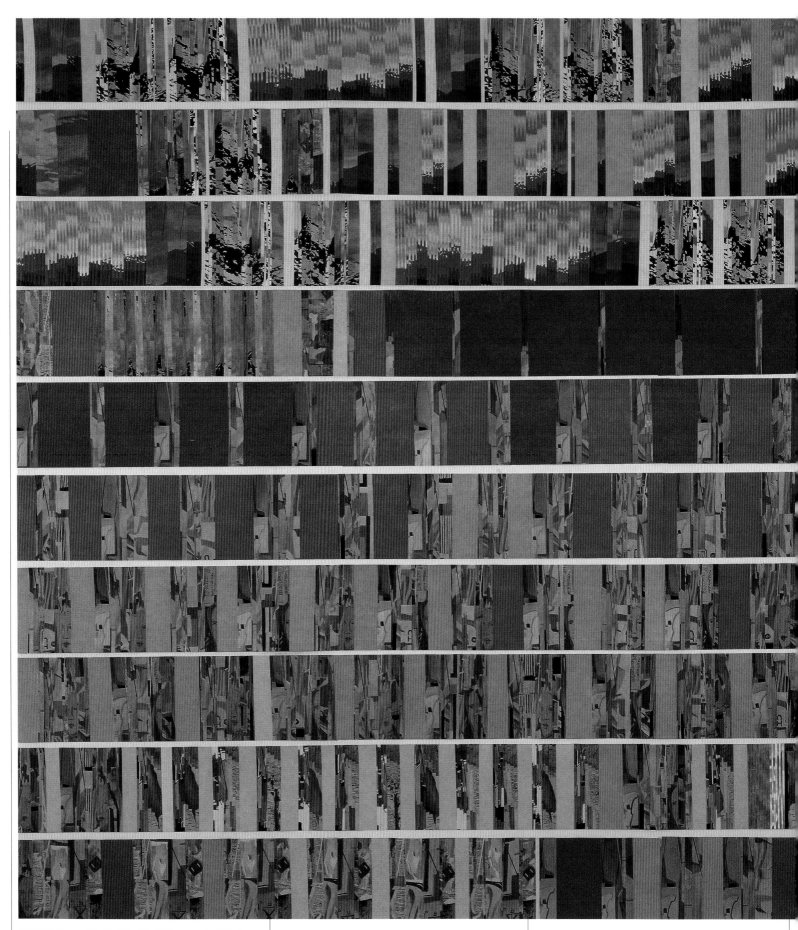

ABOVE: Second half of the First Movement of Kurt Schwitters'Ursonate as visually realized by Jack Ox. This section contains much of the Hanover Merzbau theme: **Fümms bö wö tää zää Uu, pögiff, Kwii Ee.** *Oil paint on mylar, then collaged. This section is 6m x 3m.*

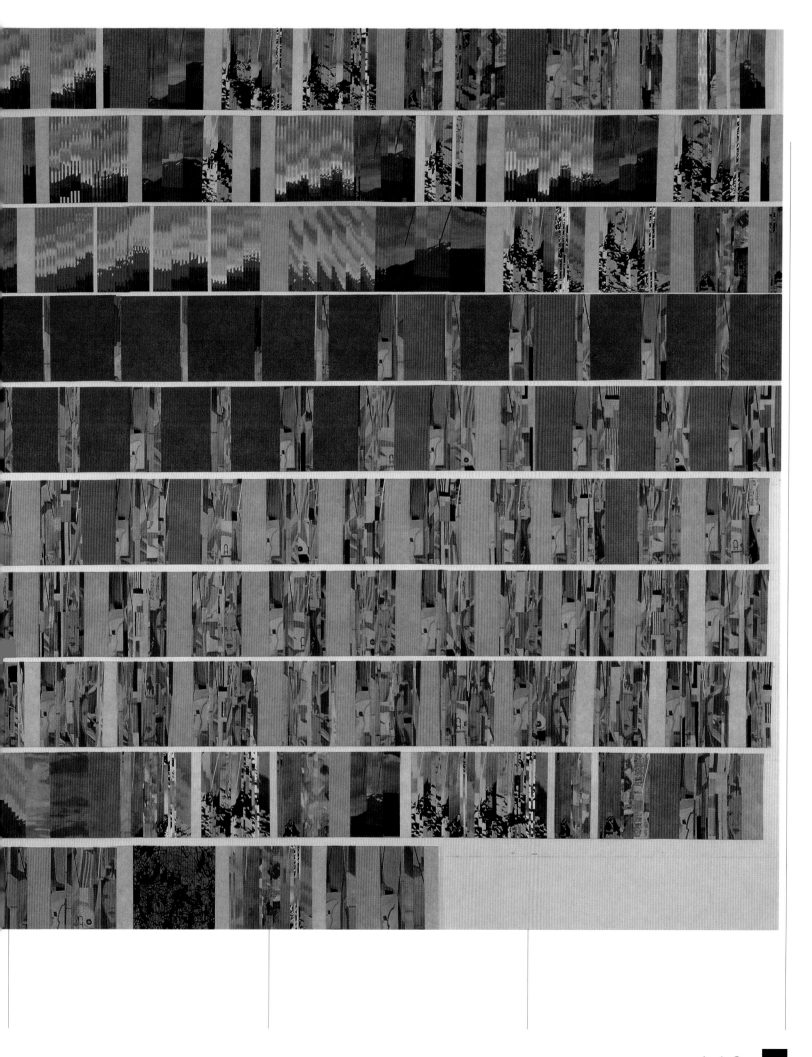

Bruce Nauman at the Pompidou

Images/Texts 1966–1996

Raw War *(1970)*
The sign consists of the single word WAR made up of a double line of coloured neon. The sequence of illumination consists of three phases: the letter R lights up alone; the letter A lights up alone; the three letters of the word WAR light up together. The word RAW, an inverted reflected image of WAR, cannot be read in the same space but is what builds and lights up into the word WAR and at the same time dissolves into it in the luminous saturation of the sign, where it disappears, except in the memory of the spectator.

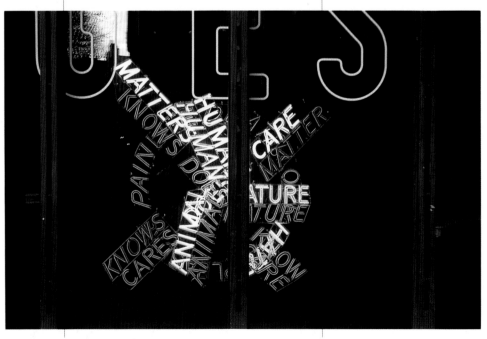

Pompidou facade with Human Nature/Life Death/Knows Doesn't Know *(1983).*
Photographs taken for NA through the windows of the Pompidou.

Bruce Nauman is the multimedia artist par excellence. His broad range of fields goes from the plastic arts, via music, dance, poetry and architecture, to the mechanical arts, including photography, audio-tape, film and video.

The fifty works done between 1966 and 1996 now on show at the Pompidou include audiovisual, sound and neon installations, drawings and photographs, organized around the themes of language, the acoustic and visual environment, and the processes of spectator participation. But, as the Pompidou points out, the curator, Christine Van Assche, has chosen to present these themes in an open and generous spirit, refusing the temptation of a more definite but more restrictive perspective.

On show are masterworks such as *Going Around the Corner Piece* (1970) and *One Hundred Live and Die* (1984) alongside sketches, preparatory studies for video performances such as the *Beckett Walk Diagram II* (1968-69), and neon signs such as *White Anger, Red Danger, Yellow Peril, Black Death* (1984); film installations from *Art Make-Up* (1967-68) to *ANTHRO/SOCIO* (1991) are presented with photo-collages and visual poems such as *Love Me Tender, Move Te Lender* (1966).

As Vincent Labaume points out in the catalogue, "Nauman's intention is to develop and enrich the physical and intellectual senses of his contemporaries, and perhaps also their moral and practical senses. The experiences by which he instructs us are lessons just as much in how to lose ourselves as in how to find ourselves, as we lose ourselves in a cacophony of luminous signs, and discover ourselves under video surveillance in a maze of corridors."

"Every work is the outcome of an experience in the course of which the artist attempts to form a question, or an idea, whose structure he reveals... The complexity of these interrogations does not however remove his work from the essential." (Christine van Assche).

Bruce Nauman, Images/Texts 1966-96 is at the South Gallery of the Pompidou Centre, rue St. Merri. All material courtesy the Pompidou Centre.

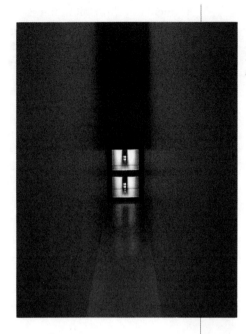

Here the artist is perhaps ironically offering an alternative to a window, purposely misplaced.

Going Around the Corner Piece *(1970). The visitor is led to walk around the outer walls of a large cubic construction, at each corner of which a video camera and a monitor are installed. But the camera is not connected to the monitor next to it - the image captured at one corner is shown at the corner directly opposite; which produces in visitors (in this case NA editorial staff) the strange sensation of seeing themselves turn round a corner and never being able to catch up with themselves.*

Hoarding showing **Rinde Spinning,** *1992. Photocollage. Triumphs over major refurbishment work at the Pompidou*

Sculptures for Bedlam
Raving and Melancholy Madness

Bethlem Royal Hospital, the world's oldest hospital for the insane, is celebrating its 750th anniversary with an exhibition at the Museum of London that reveals changing attitudes to care for the mentally ill as reflected in art and architecture.

The first Bethlem, a monastic priory in Bishopsgate in the City of London was replaced in the seventeenth century by a palatial, lavishly ornamented, building with a facade over 550 ft. long in Moorfields. But although all was serene and grand on the outside, inside was the grim, chaotic scene of William Hogarth's painting *A Rake's Progress* (1735). Bethlem is, after all, the origin of the word 'bedlam.'

Another building with a grand facade was erected in 1815 when the hospital moved from the city to St. George's Fields in Lambeth. (It is now the Imperial War Museum.) Finally, in the 1920s, Bethlem moved to a country estate where its architecture is based on the 'villa' system of small self-contained blocks set in landscaped grounds and gardens to maximise the presence of air, light and space.

The most striking exhibits at the Museum of London are the two colossal sculptures, *Raving Madness* and *Melancholy Madness*. In the words of the eminent art critic John Russell Taylor they 'deserve to be ranked among the most outstanding sculpture ever produced in this country.' For the poet Wordsworth they were 'among the greatest wonders of the capital.' The work of the Danish-born sculptor Caius Gabriel Cibber,

Raving Madness

they were erected in 1676 on the ends of a broken pediment above the elaborate piers of the gates of the Moorfields building, 14ft above the ground. They dominated the entrance for over a hundred years, reflecting for patients (who included such prominent Victorian artists as Richard Dadd and John Martin) and visitors alike the sculptor's compassionate attitude to the insane. No one passing through the gates could be indifferent to their power.

When the hospital moved to Southwark in 1815, the statues were taken down and hidden behind curtains in the entrance hall of the new building; in 1858 they were banished for another hundred years to the Victoria and Albert. Today they are proudly displayed at Bethlem's own museum.

The exhibition *Bedlam: Custody, Care and Cure* is at the Museum of London, London Wall, EC2

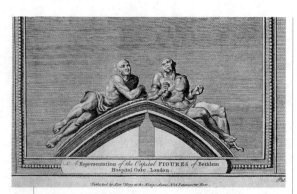

Raving and Melancholy Madness
Eighteenth-century engraving of the two stone statues on the gate posts of the second Bethlem Hospital at Moorfields. They were carved by the Danish sculptor C.G. Cribber and erected in the 1670s.

Engraving of the hospital's second building, completed in 1676 at Moorfields in the City of London. The architect was Robert Hooke (1635-1703).

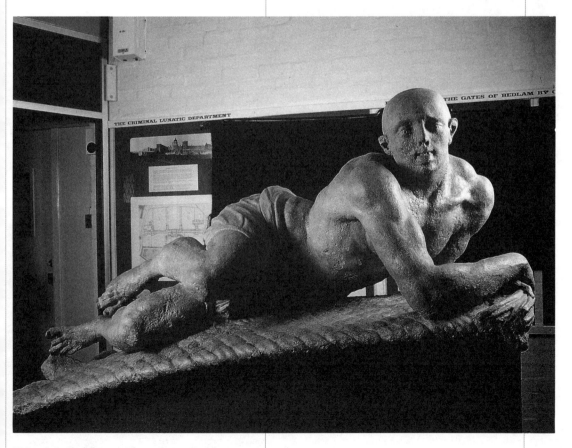

Melancholy Madness

Italian Silver

Gae Aulenti
Tea and coffee set (1979)
Cleto Munari Design Associati srl

There is today an explosion of new silver design inspired by the expressive qualities of the metal itself and the quest for innovative products. This movement, which began in Italy but has spread to the whole world of design, is imposing new codes of modernity based on creativity and logic in a sector previously anchored and idealized in the forms of the past. Amongst the leading designers who have responded to the challenge are a number of international architects.

The exhibition of 100 designs by 20 designers from 14 Italian manufacturers now touring the American Continent presents superb examples of the inventiveness of the designers and the skill of the silversmiths.

Argenti Italiani, Selezione Design, *a travelling exhibition, organized by Dessel srl and the* Italian Ministry of Foreign Affairs.

Afra / Tobia Scarpa
Carafes (1992)
San Lorenzo srl

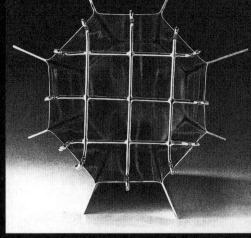

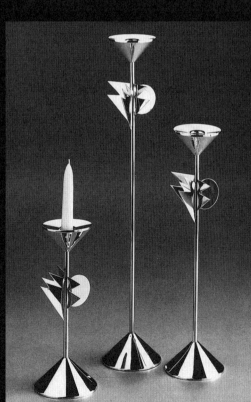

Iella and Massimo Vignelli
Striped carafe (1971)
San Lorenzo srl

Mario Botta
Carafes (1987)
Cleto Munari Design Associati srl

The Schools

The Architectural Association School of Architecture, London

This feature is the second in a continuing series on the schools which presents the best in architecture education internationally.
Whether you mention the Architectural Association in Tokyo, New York, Los Angeles or Athens, it immediately evokes architecture teaching at its most innovative at a school where distinguished architects from all over the world lecture with pleasure and where, this year alone, twenty-five exhibitions will be held, as well as numerous lectures and conferences.

The Architectural Association is Britain's oldest independent school of architecture. Established 150 years ago as a place where architects and apprentices could meet and discuss the important issues of the day, it has constantly upheld its founders' principal aim: to open up architectural practice and education to critical discussion on all levels. Its ethos and its teaching methods have been profoundly influential internationally, and today architects come from all over the world to study, work and teach in Bedford Square.

The Architectural Association recently celebrated its 150th anniversary. The celebrations were important – not just as a measure of the value of the AA's continuing contribution to architecture, but as a means of making specific histories present again.

Anniversaries of all kinds inevitably carry with them a certain degree of nostalgia, yet they are explicit reminders of what has been forgotten – left behind by the passing of time. Equally they are markers – points in time from which new events and new projects begin.

Many of the AA's 150th anniversary debates were organized expressly to articulate the conditions necessary for future projects. The relationship between education and practice, the role of criticism, and new forms of urbanism were among the many topics of discussion.

The week-long series of events raised many unanswered questions and hinted at new territories for exploration. What seems clear is that the school cannot carry on a project of 'natural' continuity with the past: rather, it must anticipate, debate, and formulate the changing roles and definitions of architecture and of architects.

The work of the AA as a forum for debate is complemented by its organizational structures, which give it the capacity to research new ideas and to respond quickly to change. A more complex architectural and urban landscape is arising out of the juxtaposition of diverse economic, social, political and cultural conditions. Under such circumstances, the limits of a project cannot be reduced to the limits of one's own culture. Consequently many of the units at the AA are becoming concerned with investigating new techniques for the configuration of architectural and urban forms which transcend the local.

It is the unpredictability of what is yet to come – the work of the students – which makes the future a challenge, a new territory.

The relationship between architectural education and architectural practice is not an easy one to unfold. In its current state, conventional architectural practice does not provide sufficient opportunities or inspiration for future architects. There are always exceptions to the rule, of course, but in the UK, as well as in many other countries, one cannot speak of a culture of architecture which offers a vision for the future. What, in this context, is the role of a school of architecture? What are its responsibilities?

The notion that a radical transformation in architecture and urbanism is possible only within a new political structure has prevailed for too long. As a result, architects have abdicated their responsibilities, acting as docile agents in the fabrication of an architecture of normalcy. It is no wonder, then, that students and schools of architecture have such an ambivalent relationship to the profession.

It may be as a reaction to the conventionality of contemporary practice that many schools have ended up marginalising themselves and their work. To some extent marginalisation provides protection – a necessary barrier – against the unacceptable aspects of main-stream practice, while in a more positive sense the shift to the periphery brings with it the textual fecundity of marginalia. But it is important to remember that the notations in the margins of a text remain dependent on their relation to that text. Similarly, if a school allows itself to become detached from the practice of architecture, its contribution to the discipline will become incomprehensible and irrelevant.

The uncritical acceptance of current practice is not an option for architectural education, but neither, despite some short term advantages, can perpetual marginalisation be accepted. The AA, with its particular brand of internationalism, is poised to construct alternative models of practice which are capable of overcoming the lethargy of the profession.

Instead of waiting for politics to transform everyday life, its task should be one of constructing alternative architectural visions that will provide the inspiration for further political action.

This must be the responsibility of the AA: to foster more constructive and optimistic work that is based on a re-assessment of the relationship between architectural imaginings and social possibilities. The projects shown on the followings pages are, if not wholly, at least a partial manifestation of this desire.

The school has approximately 500 students drawn from 50 countries and around 150 academic, administrative and technical staff, who are supported by specialist contributors. In addition, internationally recognized architects and scholars visit the AA to give lectures and to participate in workshops.

Courses are divided into two main areas: the undergraduate programmes, leading to the AA Diploma; and the Graduate School, which grants the AA Graduate Diploma, MA, MPhil and PhD degrees. These programmes are supplemented by the Open Unit/Foundation course, Visiting Students programme, and part-time postgraduate courses in Environmental Access, Conservation, and Professional Practice.

UNDERGRADUATE PROGRAMMES
The AA Diploma programmes comprise First Year, Intermediate School [Second and Third Year] and Diploma School [Fourth and Fifth Year]. The school has evolved a unit system which allows divergent ideas about architecture and teaching to be pursued. Urbanism, landscape, materials, technologies of produc-

tion, and the reclamation of industrial and military sites were only some of the topics explored last year in relation to specific sites in Manchester, Venice, Liverpool, London, Turin and Bombay. The wide range of sites connotes something of the internationalism of the school; the equally wide range of topics reflects the diversity that is nurtured by the unit system and given public expression through debates, juries, reviews, and other forms of open discussion.

The design-based work of the units is reinforced by the courses in General, Media, and Technical Studies. General Studies provides lectures, workshops and discussions which relate to architectural theory, practice and history, to contemporary urbanism, and to wider cultural issues. Media Studies teaches the different techniques of communication, with courses that range from drawing and model-making to the digital image and electronic media. Technical studies is concerned with the technical education of the architect: with building construction, structures, materials, environmental science, with the philosophy of technology and emergent technologies. These resources are available equally to students in the Graduate School.

Besides the AA Diploma programmes, two further options are available at undergraduate level. The Visiting Students programme gives students from other schools world-wide the opportunity to participate in the academic and cultural life of the AA for one year, while the Open Unit/Foundation course offers an explanatory learning environment in which students may freely develop their ideas about architecture.

GRADUATE PROGRAMMEs
The Graduate School offers one-year MA courses and MPhil and PhD research degrees in the areas of Environment and Energy, Histories and Theories of Architecture, and Housing and Urbanism. It also offers eighteen-month studio-based AA Graduate Diploma courses in Architecture and Urban Design [the DRL] and in Landscape Architecture and Urbanism. While students are required to work in their chosen specialization, they are encouraged to participate in the courses offered by other Graduate programmes and by General Studies.

The AA's part-time postgraduate course in Environmental Access – the first qualification in this subject from any institution – brings together students involved in the planning, design and implementation necessary to create an environment accessible to all. Other postgraduate courses are devoted to Building Conversation, Historic Landscape and Garden Conservation, and Professional Practice.

All of these activities are based at the AA's premises in Bedford Square, central London, in a Georgian building enhanced by facilities such as the Exhibition Gallery, the Library, the Triangle Bookshop, the Photo Library, the Materials Shop, Bar and Members' Room.

Fredrik Walin
Dismembering Scheme

Site: Ex US Airforce base, Upper Heyford, Oxfordshire, UK

Open the damp void after the F 1-11 to address the aspiration of a new epoch – allow progressing demolition to act as a productive source. Where the gradual decapacitation not only liberates the recyclable inner steel shell and landfill materials, but also creates wind-protected yards suitable for tree nurseries – trees after they have gained strength, can be transferred out on site as structuring, zoning and windbreaking elements.
The pictured sequence shows a proposal for the demolition of a hangar. A study of possible demolition techniques culminated in the description of possible stable phases of partial demolition. Proposed removal of all structures above a level of 3.5m results in the creation of a rectangular walled garden – a tree nursery sheltered from the worst exposures of the base's hilltop site.

Ludo Grooteman
Complex Icon

House project
Site: Spitalfields Market, London, UK

Site

The project is located west of the Spitalfields Market in London. This area is called the City Fringe, mainly because it borders the City of London and the Brick Lane area. Over the last five years the state of the neighbourhood has been the concern of two organizations: the Bethnal Green City Challenge, a subsidised organization whose aim is to 'put the area back on its feet;' and the Spitalfields Development Group, whose aim is to redevelop the area and replace most of its existing buildings – including a large part of the market – with corporate offices and housing. The Spitalfields Market is the focal point of the re-establishment strategy of the Bethnal Green City Challenge, and functions as a zone of highly dynamic heterogeneous activity and occupation.

Strategy

The research focused on the urban quality offered by the area's flexible border condition; a highly heterogeneous definition and use. The building on the site is intended to continue the complex organization of the City Fringe when the City Fringe ceases to exist.

The Mini Motel Market: An interconnection of diverse and differently privileged participants – market, inhabitants, and City – into one point. The Mini Motel Market provides market living and market working [pay per hour] within the pre-existing facilities of Spitalfields Market.

Programme

The MMM is an urban machine capable of adapting to different requirements and times of the day. The programme for the MMM is dynamic. The public programme, the engine of the MMM, is determined. The market programme will be mainly active during the day. During the night and the early morning living/working units can fully expand.

Space

In order to make space flexible and adaptable, all utilities are located in containers. From these containers the flexible spaces literally unfold. The Mini Motel Market is developed by means of the simulation of five typical spaces: i.e. the roof unit that unfolds upwards and has its utilities compressed in the bottom space; the minimum unit that can either be retracted to form a 3sq.m fully equipped living unit, or folded out to provide a 25sq.m living/working space; plus the linking unit that can be expanded over four units, adding spaces and functions.

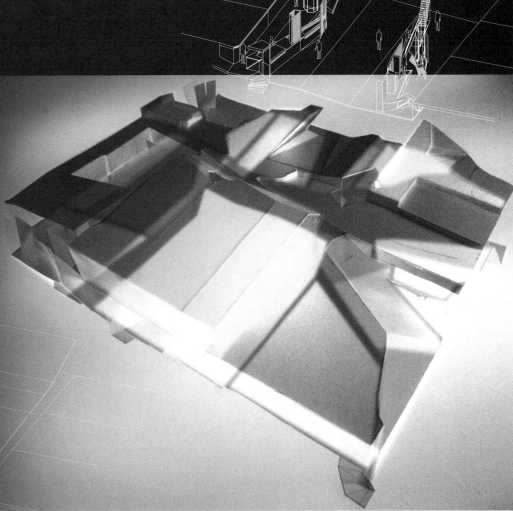

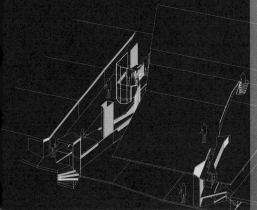

Valis   Loizides
Urban Chorgeography
Honours diploma

House project
Site: Lahti, Finland

Urban chorgeography
A paradigmatic shift from the centre as a static point towards multitudinous coexisting mobile points, challenges hierarchical staticity on multiple scales. The goal is to unfold new forms of temporal coexistence from the collision of local systems within a global field and to fabricate dynamic field relations to oscillate between various scales. Each point of intensity exists with a maximum degree of comfort within a group of points and is always ready to connect, allowing the potential of the unplanned to unfold.

Metamorphic space
The house destabilizes organizational hierarchies while articulating and activating its space as a field of shifting territorial conditions. The pattern of occupation and activities changes continuously and leaves no trace of its short-time territories. The house is not an assemblage of secluded units but rather a continuous spatial transition. Its transparent space enables maximum integration and interaction of its utilizations at any time. Perhaps it can be described as a reassembling unit which reconfigures its mobile components within its unrestrained frame, guided by its adaptation to the occupants' requirements and its involvement with the external forces of the site.

Tectonics
A single-surface and self-supporting steel structure forms a continuous band that loops vertically. Together with interlinked horizontally looping glass panels, it delivers manifold degrees of enclosure. Two curtains interfere with the opening and closing of the glass panels. One is made of a steel thread fabric, the other one is woven of light-emitting fibres. The curtains' configuration organizes short-time multiple-use requirements while leaving space for different degrees of independence to coexist within the same territory.

Shifting intensities
1. time: multiple short-time activities – tv, library, dining , leisure, working, etc.
    1. arrangement: curtains divide level I spaces into smaller territories serving activity and access requirements; one space accommodates multifarious activities and returns to its wholeness
    2. time: public event – entrance, cloakroom, catering, open public space, etc.
    2. arrangement: two minor curtain divisions, use of entire level I space, mobile furniture removal to remaining private territory; continuity of interior to exterior space
    3. time: increased privacy activities: sleeping, bathing, study, etc.
    3. arrangement: curtains divide parts of level I and the whole of level II into several private territories; mobile furniture positioning is coordinated with curtain divisions.

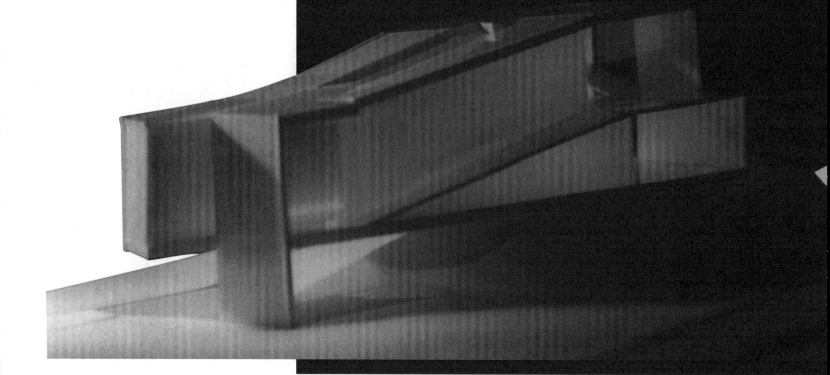

Christopher C.M. Lee
Woven Organization

*House project
site: Spitalfields Market, London, UK*

Strategy
The site of the project is an empty site next to Spitalfields Market. The market houses constantly shifting activities with a wide variety of visitors and users. At weekends the market is filled with activities that are visually rich and constantly shifting. Unknown to most of the market users is the Spitalfields Arts Project that houses more than seventy artists in the basement of the market, the production and products of these artists are barely known or seen by the market users. The intention is to make the production and products of art more apparent within the visual field of the urban fabric; and to utilize the resultant effects to strengthen the political voice of the artist community against developer-driven interests.

Woven potential I
Visual fields were mapped out on the site from key locations, and the ground plane was folded to accommodate new visual and physical continuities and connections. The planes form a continuous surface that organizes movement and directs visual perception. Three event structures were determined with reference to the users of the market and the visual field of the existing and the new spaces: exhibiting, living and working. The living programme offers temporary living for the artist working in the studios and the proposed studios are linked to the existing studios in the basement of the market. Activities that relate to the three event structures are distributed with reference to their location within the visual field, the angles of inclined surfaces and degree of visibility of the surfaces. These activities weave into one another together with the surface direction and inclination.

Woven potential II
Inclined surfaces weave new visual fields from above the ground plane towards the -7.5m level, and allow the observer and the market user to encounter art as an event that accompanies the events in the market. The art is viewed under one's feet, over one's head or multiplicitously as one passes through the site to and from the market. The project employs primarily two materials, concrete and glass. The intention is for the gallery entry mass to be as visually permeable as possible to enhance the effect of the extended visual field. The field seemingly collapses into the space of the project and draws movement flow towards the lower spaces.

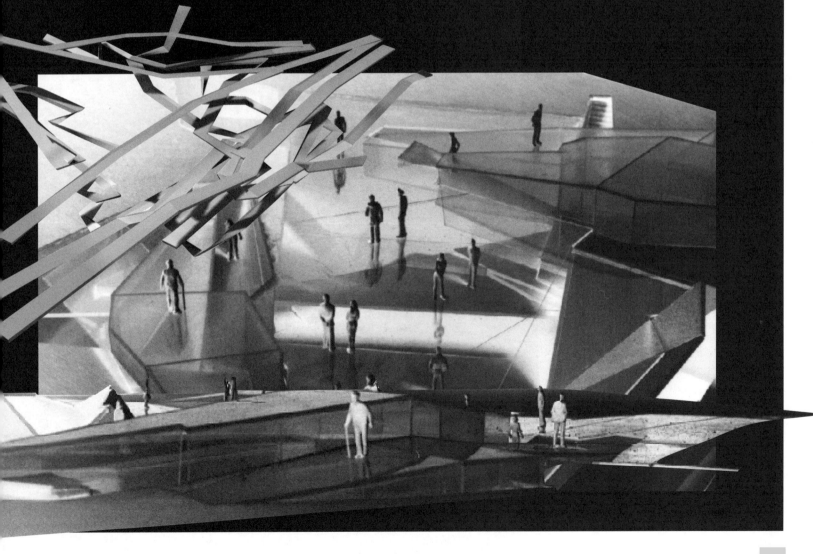

Yoon King Chong
Movement, velocity and field

House project – the Plastic House
Site: Spitalfields Market, London, UK

Corb colour fields
The initial analysis focused on Le Corbusier's paintings, which were interpreted as two juxtaposed systems of colour and zonal/thematic fields, which both remain internally disjointed and incongruent in the organization of their distinct components.

Field
Movement and velocity initialize local points of intensities and densities within undetermined field conditions. Local points of intensification condense zones of complex transition from one velocity to another or from one mode of circulation to another. Movement is at once the potential for intensification and connectivity, as local points of intensification are interconnected by mobile routing systems from one point to another and amongst all points as shifting network relations.

Pliant continuity
The spatial organization is both continuous and discontinuous, similar and dissimilar as a transition space that unfolds continuous new permutations of movement to activity pattern related to changes of velocities on undulating surfaces. Space is conceived as transitional relations rather than a static condition.

Malleable programme
A stereotypical and static programme has been dispensed with in favour of a dynamic pliant activity distribution. This distribution is perpetually being renegotiated in relation to the diverse active and inactive movement loops within the terrain and the degree of transparency of the undulating surfaces.

Synthetics
Plastic house is made of glass fibre reinforced plastic. The complex curved surfaces consist of pre-fabricated sandwich sections. S-glass fibre reinforcement delivers high strength performance, bearing tensile, compressive and shear forces. Pigment fillers are used to achieve translucency and opacity of surfaces.

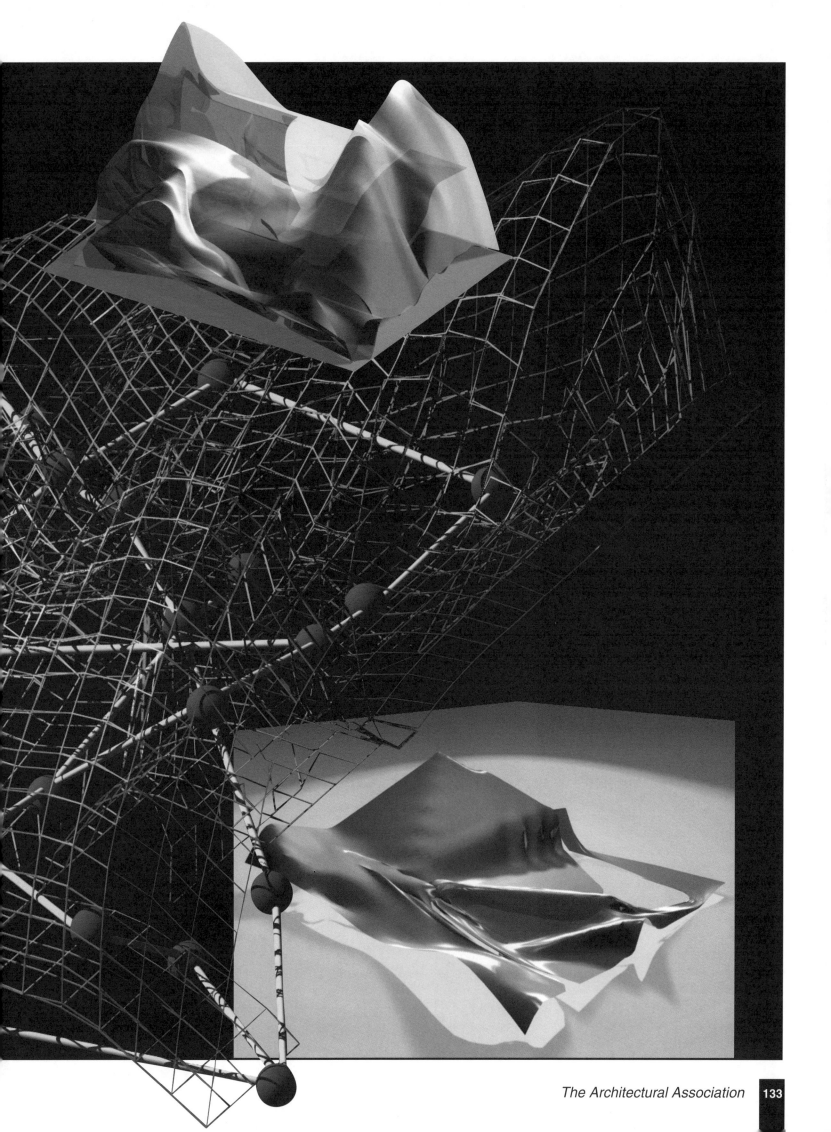

Ben Marston
Citylandscape

Synthetic urban geology
Site: Docklands in Southwark, London, UK

The site is a regenerated area typical of many redeveloped dockyards in London's east end. Extensive redevelopment occurred in the 1980s but the economic recession of the 1990s left large areas undeveloped, their communities disparate and not connected to the social housing surrounding the site.

The thesis is an attempt to create a coherent fabric. The hypothesis is that characteristics of the surrounding urban fabric and topography can be used to generate, through a process of anamorphic transformation, a new landscape of potential in this urban void. The intent is that by generating an urban geology which is an abstracted construct of surrounding topographic conditions, the communities might be connected, and that the spatial conditions proposed can be colonized as a town centre.

The thesis proposes that town centres are no longer perceived as a determined series of programmatic elements but as a colonization of an existing topography. For example, many banks are closing branches which are colonized as restaurants as the nature of society and the way we live evolves.

But in this site there is no existing topography: it is effectively an undeveloped void. Is it possible to synthesize these topographical conditions to generate an urban geology of potential for this colonization to occur?

Reading the city like an inhabited piece of geology, scans were made of the surrounding topographic conditions, identifying and measuring qualities of the context. This information was then translated into the void of the site using techniques of anamorphic transformation, generating abstracted 'shadows' of topographic codings into the interior, creating overlaps between specific topographic conditions. In the exterior conditions of the topography are discreet; in the interior projections they become mixed.

These new projections or layers of strata read in a new way, not configured into a conventional built form, but more into a geological topography that allows occupation of space to occur in new ways.

Laurence Liauw
KLSC Mixed Use Masterprogramme

Site: Kuala Lumpur, Malaysia

Kuala Lumpur is currently in the process of shifting from a monocentric structure to becoming a dispersed polycentric city. KLSC will be a new 200 acre centre on a tabula rasa site serving a catchment of 250,000 people. A new paradigm of '3D Mixing' is deployed to generate urban diversity and density. Four external cities sampled for their organizational/programmatic properties, are topologically projected back to the empty site and negotiated with local constraints. Overlapping programmes occur both in plan and section at multiple scales. Blurring of generic categories opens up new spatial possibilities. KLSC will be developed in phases to incorporate infrastructure, demographic and market fluctuations. The universal acquires specificity, as it becomes an artifi- cially engineered quilt of urban hybrids.

Kate Darby
Light Extraction (minus 80 million tonnes)

Site: the isle of Portland

Portland is an island that is quarried. This project is concerned with the shifting void that arises from quarrying and proposals to measure and intervene in this process.

The aesthetic (rock) pulling device is designed to create order within a disordered landscape. It is a pulley attached to two stones simultaneously, force is applied in the centre and the lighter stone moves towards the heavier one. This tool creates a set of rules dictated by the length of the rope; the number of blocks, the maximum weight capacity of the rope and the strength of the user. When these rules are applied to the landscape they respond to the topography to produce a pattern. A pulley is an alchemical device, given enough time, rope and blocks all the stone could be moved by hand.

Portland is an island of voids and potential voids. Here this phenomenon is examined in terms of its opposite, light. The voids that once contained stone are now each day filled and emptied of light.

The 'reading room on the edge' is an instrument to monitor this moving shadow. It is a solar edge alignment device. It makes a visual connection between a square of light cast on the ground or on a screen and the edge of the cliff that is casting the shadow. The light passes down the tube for one hour. Like the sundial it is a measure of the passing of absolute time. The moving shadow is viewed against a backdrop of frozen time past. The strata represent 20 million years of the Jurassic period.

The reading rooms or aligning devices would be placed in all the quarries to enable a measured registration of the displacement of ground over time; and to dictate the position of the infill through making visual connections and sun alignments. The objects would be made of frames that act simultaneously as light apertures and as windows.

By making visual connections between the new quarried surfaces and the edge, all around the island, perhaps one can begin to suggest new ways of inhabiting new surfaces on the island when quarrying ceases in 2042.

Chen Da Lee
Casting the boundary

Site: the isle of Portland

In the example of casting we may ask where does memory lie, in the mould or in the cast? Casting, one of the most ancient of industrial techniques, is the core of this proposal. It is a metaphorical surgical act on the land, re-profiling, lifting, shifting boundaries. Like surgery it is a delicate task, surgery for the body of the earth, but records, memorizes rather than repairs. Infrastructures forming new circulation are constructed through the following procedures:

1. *applying the jig*
2. *reinforcement*
3. *facial [surface] casting*
4. *partial removal of sedimentary layers*
5. *propping*
6. *relocating layers into a line or surface*

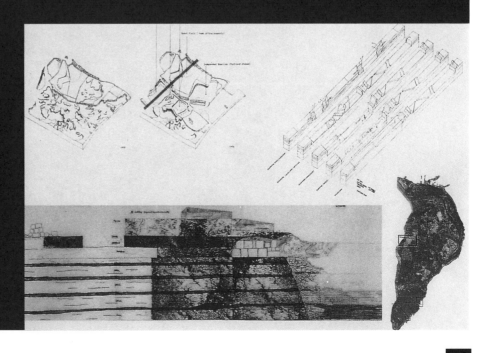

Chen Te Wo
Gap

Site: the isle of Portland

In contrast to the barbarity of the quarrying there are particular activities that have no ambition to alter the landscape but are more concerned with the body and its relation to the earth, directly confronting the elements or surface conditions and gravity. Bird-watching, riding, climbing, hang-gliding, all alter one's perception of the land without manipulating it, providing new relations between geology, weather, and patterns of transitory occupation. Like the creature who inhabits the crack in the stone, so this architecture gingerly sits, intrudes into the land's voids and gaps.

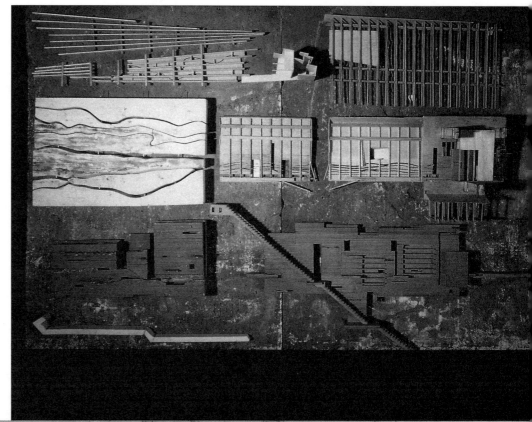

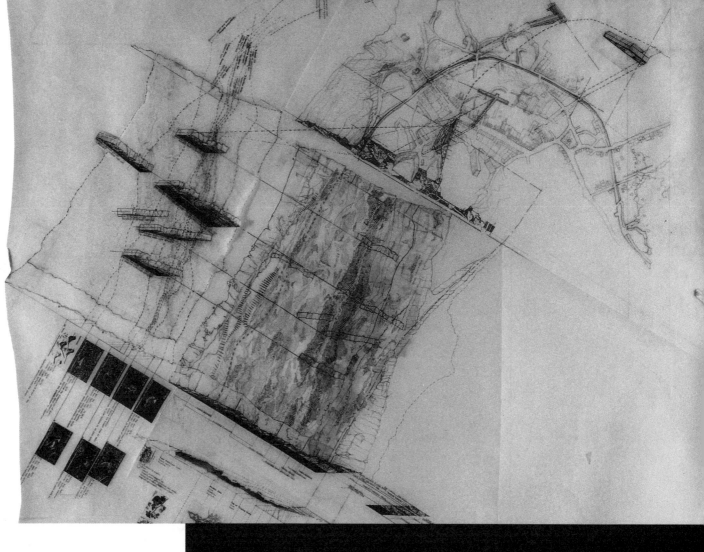

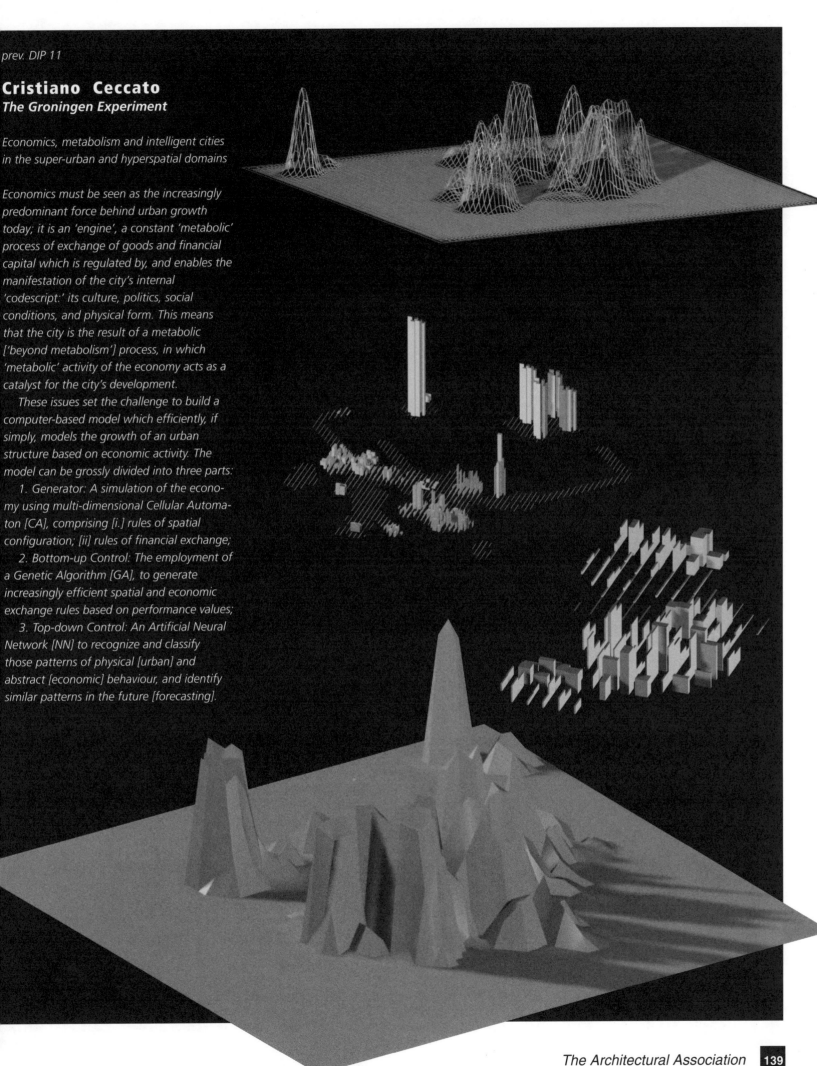

prev. DIP 11

Cristiano Ceccato
The Groningen Experiment

Economics, metabolism and intelligent cities in the super-urban and hyperspatial domains

Economics must be seen as the increasingly predominant force behind urban growth today; it is an 'engine', a constant 'metabolic' process of exchange of goods and financial capital which is regulated by, and enables the manifestation of the city's internal 'codescript:' its culture, politics, social conditions, and physical form. This means that the city is the result of a metabolic ['beyond metabolism'] process, in which 'metabolic' activity of the economy acts as a catalyst for the city's development.

    These issues set the challenge to build a computer-based model which efficiently, if simply, models the growth of an urban structure based on economic activity. The model can be grossly divided into three parts:

    1. Generator: A simulation of the economy using multi-dimensional Cellular Automaton [CA], comprising [i.] rules of spatial configuration; [ii] rules of financial exchange;

    2. Bottom-up Control: The employment of a Genetic Algorithm [GA], to generate increasingly efficient spatial and economic exchange rules based on performance values;

    3. Top-down Control: An Artificial Neural Network [NN] to recognize and classify those patterns of physical [urban] and abstract [economic] behaviour, and identify similar patterns in the future [forecasting].

prev. DIP 11

Gianni Botsford
The Groningen Experiment

Solar logic

When I stand still, I am moving

We exist in a universe full of constant
motion. The apparent motion of the sun in
our sky is caused by our movement around
the sun, creating a series of dynamic geometrical relationships from which complexity
emerges. As a result of this each point on
earth has a unique relationship with the sun.
And yet, there are constant elements within
this flux.

The model sees the sun as a generator of
form and organization in the context of an
approach to architecture that embraces the
geometrical intelligence of nature and
follows the strategies and rules that nature
has found to make best uses of its resources.
It is a generic model developed for all
latitudes and all times. The aim of the model
is to describe a three-dimensional space
consisting of points which are intelligent,
conscious, and aware of their environment,
the points around them, and their dynamic
and ever-changing relationship with the sun
and with time. This space will be able to
adapt, react, and behave through its awareness. Dynamic form and structure will
emerge for all latitudes on earth that are
responsive to that relationship and the
different states for those points dependent
on their unique contextual condition.

Global-local and local-global
This model works both with the local and
global rules of relationships. In the 'real'
world global rules apply and govern the
behaviour of the points of the datastructure.
The rules for growth are 'filtered' through
several levels of economic, sensory and

cultural opacity. The points in the datastructure have true geometrical intelligence. The results are dynamic, responsive, and inherently organic. In the 'abstract' world, local rules test for state, efficiency and neighbourhood rules of relationship. These states affect each point's growth and the future state of all other points within the datastructure as it is continuously updated, and create a means by which information can flow from the 'real' world to the abstract world within the model.

The global and local rules are subdivided into four further relationships:
- global-global [sun to earth, planet to planet, city to city, global rules sent globally];
- global-local [real world interaction with global rules at a local scale, global rules sent locally];
- local-global [local rules that have global influence, local rules sent globally];
- local-local [logic fields, rules of neighbourhood, local rules sent locally].

These deal with the varying intensity of the relationship with the other models interacting with the central model and locally with the solar system, as well as categorizing the influence and effect that can be established between the networks and their relationships.

Jacques Derrida and Peter Eisenman
CHORA L WORKS
Edited by Jeffrey Kipnis and Thomas Leeser, 212 pp., ill., some colour, The Monacelli Press, New York, PB £37.50, US$55
Discussion transcripts, candid correspondence, and essays, sketches, presentation drawings and models documenting the collaboration between philosopher Jacques Derrida and architect Peter Eisenman on a project for the Parc de la Villette in Paris. The design process was guided by Plato's *chora* text from the *Timeaus*.

THE FORM OF JAPANESE WINDOWS
Essays by Fumihiko Maki, Tetsuro Kurokawa, Kunihiro Ando, Koji Yagi and Ayako Nakamura, 200pp., ill., Flat Glass Manufacturers Association of Japan, HB.
An examination of the characteristics of the windows born from the history, geography and lifestyles of Japan, and the ideas of the people that made them, revealing how Japanese architectural culture developed and changed through the ages.

Pascal and Maria Maréchau
IMPRESSIONS OF YEMEN
200pp, lavishly illustrated in colour, Flammarion, HB, £37.50 US$55
A beautiful book on a culture threatened by modern technology which nevertheless demonstrates a mastery of materials, tools and symbols to produce a polychrome architecture of immense and lasting power.

Arakawa and Madeline Gins
REVERSIBLE DESTINY -
We Have Decided Not To Die
Introductions by Michael Govan and Jean-François Lyotard, 324pp., ill. in colour, Guggenheim Museum/Harry N. Abrams Inc., HB, £48, US$75
Mammoth catalogue of the 1997 exhibition at the Guggenheim Museum. Exploring a range of perspectives from biology to cognitive science and employing such diverse mediums as drawing, painting, sculpture, poetry, architecture and city planning, Arakawa and Gins remain committed to pushing language and art beyond aesthetics towards an entire philosophy of living and being. Their work will be featured in the next number of NEW ARCHITECTURE.

John Hejduk
PEWTER WINGS, GOLDEN HORNS, STONE VEILS
Edited by Kim Shkapich, 304pp, 200 ills., 180 in colour, The Monacelli Press, pb, £27/US$40
An architectural journey/novel traversing a mental/physical landscape of architectural sites, churches, chapels and cathedrals, influenced by Spain. The seven chapters – Crossings, Sites, Rituals, Wedding in a Dark Plum Room, Sacraments, Testaments, and Journeys – are accompanied by watercolours and ink drawings.

John Hejduk
ADJUSTING FOUNDATIONS
Edited by Kim Shkapich, 224pp, 200 colour ills., The Monacelli Press, pb, £25/US$35
A provocative collection of deeply personal drawings and writings that explore the relationship between the still life of the painter and the work of the architect. A series of watercolours that are cubist in spirit gives birth to sixty-one project proposals, including serpentine structures, secret spaces, a nd houses constructed of horizontal and vertical mazes.

Lee Goff
STONE BUILT: Contemporary American Houses
Introduction by Charles Gwathmey, 272pp., illus. in colour, The Monacelli Press, HB, £40/US$60
The twenty-seven houses documented here lead Goff to conclude that a renaissance of stone houses is at hand. She discusses the design of each house with the architect, focusing on the decision to use stone and the building process. Colour photographs of both interiors and exteriors complete the story.

Richard Meier
BARCELONA MUSEUM OF CONTEMPORARY ART
Introduction by Dennis L. Dollens, Essay by Richard Meier, and Afterword by Federico Correa, 96pp., ill. in colour, The Monacelli Press, PB, £19.99/US$29.95
"I'm not saying this is a great work of art, but I'm out to make it a work of art. It's a museum, a cathedral of our time. ... Today a museum is more than a container for works of art. ... It's a place where people come together, a social place as well as a place for contemplation," stated Richard Meier to the *New York Times*. Dollens speculates that MACBA is one of Meier's finest buildings, one that could easily be considered in an honoured position on a time line between New Harmony and the Getty Center – a signature building and a landmark.

Margaret Henderson Floyd
HENRY HOBSON RICHARDSON:
A Genius for Architecture
Photographs by Paul Rocheleau, 304pp, ill. in colour, The Monacelli Press, HB, £50/US$75.
Architectural historian Margaret Henderson Floyd reassesses Richardson's relationship to his own epoch, his method, his influence on subsequent architectural developments, and his unique architectural fusions, in which he synthesized eclectic sources as allusions across time and culture. Rocheleau's colour photographs, combined with a large number of archival images, present a new vision of the architect's oeuvre and reveal his genius for architecture.

Christophe Canto, Odile Falin
THE HISTORY OF THE FUTURE
Images of the 21st Century
160pp. ill. in col. and B&W, Flammarion, hb, £35/US$45
A time machine in which the authors comb the pas from the 1850s to the 1950a in search of a fabulous future that inspired both fear and reverence. Illustrations include postcards, comics, science fiction and the cinema from Fritz Lang to modern classics.

Jean-Louis Cohen
SCENES OF THE WORLD TO COME
European Architecture and the American Challenge 1893-1960
224pp, over 200 ills, Flammarion, pb, £28/US$45
A perceptive study of the European discovery of the North American city with its grand hotels, skyscrapers, and massive industrial plants; and of its infatuatjion with domestic applicances and mechanization.

Daniel Libeskind
RADIX–MATRIX
Essays by Jacques Derrida and Mark C. Taylor, 168pp, ill. in colour, Prestel, HB, £39.95/ US$65
A unique attempt to provide a comprehensive critical analysis of Libeskind's architecture and philosophy. The architect serves as mediator of his own work, exploring various projects through an illuminating juxtaposition of textual commentary with illustrations of competition models, concept drawings, and site photographs of realized works.

Ed. Annette Becker, John Olley and Wilfried Wang
20TH CENTURY ARCHITECTURE IN IRELAND
200pp., ill. in colour, Prestel/ Deutsches Architektur-Museum, HB, £39.95/US$65
An extensive survey of Ireland's 20th century architecture presenting over 50 buildings in detail with photographs and original design drawings. A series of essays examines the influence of Irish literature, politics and national identity on the country's architecture.

Alvaro Siza
SIZA - ARCHITECTURE WRITINGS
Edited by Antonio Angelillo, 208pp., b&w, Skira, £15.95
Part of the series Theories and Works of Contemporary Architects which offers a panorama of the vast legacy of theoretical writings by modern and contemporary architects while providing a tool for reflection on design and on the salient themes of international architecture. A useful bibliography is included.

Anne Baldassari
PICASSO AND PHOTOGRAPHY: The Dark Mirror
264pp, ill b&w and colour, Flammarion/Museum of Fine Arts, Houston, HB, £40/US$55
Picasso's appetite for experimentation led him to push photography to unorthodox extremes, resulting in independent works of art: superimposed photographs, cliché-verres, photo-based engravings, photograms and original drawings on photographs, slides, collages and photographic cut-outs.

ORDER FORM

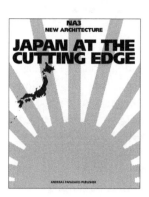

NEW ARCHITECTURE SUBSCRIPTION RATES FOR SIX ISSUES		
Full rate	£90.00	US$135
Students	£60.00	US$ 90

YES! I wish to subscribe to NEW ARCHITECTURE   £.........   US$.........

I wish to order the following books:

..... NA1 - Reaching for the Future	£17.50	US$27.50
..... NA2 - The End of Innovation in Architecture	£17.50	US$27.50
..... NA3 - Japan at the Cutting Edge	£17.50	US$27.50
..... Architecture: Choice or Fate by Léon Krier	£24.95	US$39.00
..... Classical Architecture by Demetri Porphyrios	£19.50	US$35.00
..... NA Monographs: Peter Pran	£22.50	US$37.50
..... Promotion of Architecture by Sebastian Loew	£ 7.95	US$12.00
..... The Art of Glass by Victor Arwas	£17.50	US$35.00

I enclose cheque/money order/bank draft for

Please charge £........ to my credit card

Account No.

Expiry date

Signature

NAME and ADDRESS

ANDREAS PAPADAKIS PUBLISHER

Kilbees Farm, Windsor Forest, Berks SL4 2EH, UK   Tel. +44 (0)13 44 88 20 40   Fax +44 (0)13 44 88 20 41

Cumulative Index

The prefix indicates the number of the issue in which the work appears:

1 - NA1 REACHING FOR THE FUTURE
2 - NA2 THE END OF INNOVATION IN ARCHITECTURE
Extensive presentation is indicated in bold.